CHURCH IS FAMILY

Becoming More of Who We Are

an in-depth New Testament study by

Graeme C. Young

Grosvenor House
Publishing Limited

i

The right of Graeme C. Young to be identified as the author of this
work has been asserted in accordance with Section 78
of the Copyright, Designs and Patents Act 1988

The Book cover is copyright to Graeme C. Young,
Cover image credit: Dmitry Lobanov

This book is published by
Grosvenor House Publishing Ltd
Link House
140 The Broadway, Tolworth, Surrey, KT6 7HT.
www.grosvenorhousepublishing.co.uk

A CIP record for this book
is available from the British Library

ISBN 978-1-80381-223-6
eBook ISBN 978-1-80381-224-3

CONTENTS

CHURCH IS FAMILY - AN INTRODUCTION

1. CHURCH IS FAMILY – WHY IS THIS IMPORTANT?

- In the past generation in the UK there have been many people leaving their involvement in a local church because of either a lessening of commitment, changing circumstances, or the feeling that "church" is not doing or being what it is meant to do and be. There is not now the continuity of generation to generation connection with church that there has been in families in previous generations. There have also been people leaving local church, not because they are less committed as Christians, but because they are questioning the relevance of their church's activities and relationship structures to them living for Jesus and seeking to help others to follow Him.

- The place and involvement of children in church life has been a major part of my ministry, and Church being Family is central to that. I have had the privilege of seeing the understanding of church as family and the involvement of children expressed really well in many congregations for whom it meant a changed mindset and relationships. Others still struggle with this area, and a greater understanding of "Church is Family" would help them.

- Organisational structures of church congregations and denominations/ groups/ streams can mask the reality of church being family, or at times stand contrary to that understanding.

- The place and function of church "leaders", in the many varied forms that takes in differing church styles, is how churches often define themselves. Some forms of leadership are more compatible than others to church being a family relationship.

- In churches where the activities are based on just a congregational service or two a week, there is a lack of the kind of shared life which is conducive to growth. As a pastor mentioned following a conversation at a newly started prayer breakfast, "I realised that I've been in the same church as these guys for ten years, and I don't know their testimony."

- Society is becoming increasingly characterised by fatherless children, whether by the parents' deliberate lifestyle choice, or by the unintended consequence of a casual relationship, or by the lack of commitment of the father to their child and the child's mother, or the separation resulting from his abuse of them. The resulting prevalence of behavioural, mental health and self-worth difficulties are clear for anyone who has an eye to see. This is compounded by there now being not only fatherless children, but also a growing generation of fatherless parents, who in their own childhood were denied the experience of their father, and who missed the educational patterning of relationships that comes from growing up in a setting where not only are they loved by a parent, but they experience and learn from the loving relationship that their parents have with each another. Related to this is the ever growing confusion of personal identity, "Who am I?" and "Where do I belong?" with the ongoing invention of new categories in an ever more complicated attempt to define satisfactory answers to unsatisfied hearts.

If "Church is Family" is being rightly lived out in the life of the church, then we have something to offer to the multitudes who are family-deprived, and who, whether they recognise it or not, are longing for that which is found in true family. We have the possibility – and responsibility - to so demonstrate family relationship in the Church Family that it will be an example to individuals and families to learn from and follow in the building or rebuilding of their own family relationships and lifestyle. Perhaps the extent to which such family-deprived people are looking to the church is a sign of our strength or weakness in this area.

- Adding to the difficulties of society has been one after another of the historic denominations setting aside their previously held Biblical doctrines on family life, and leaving a confusion of blurred definitions of family relationships.

- For many years I have been looking forward to, and as far as I can, preparing for coming Revival. I have read of and been inspired by the multiple breakthroughs of heaven 1859-1923 into the area where I grew up on the north east coast of Scotland. While I am not expecting that any present or future moves of the Holy Spirit will simply repeat the previous experiences in the same way, revival history has shown me what can happen when many people give their lives to Jesus in a short space of time, and whole communities and churches are changed as a result. The question arises: How will traditional church respond to an influx of people who are unlikely to relate culturally or spiritually to the completely unfamiliar historic sub-cultures of the various denominations and non-denominations? How will they experience "family" in those contexts? And when, no doubt, new churches/fellowships will arise as fresh expressions of church, how much will they simply repeat historic patterns, or find more relevant ways to express that "Church is Family"?

- Then in the process of writing have come the forced changes of church life brought about by the restrictions imposed to combat the Coronavirus pandemic. Suddenly, things that were never allowed to be changed or moved have for some time gone, and churches have had to reappraise what "church" means, when their previous stable expressions of church life have had to stop. While some have simply tried to replicate their church services online, there has been an outburst of multifaceted creativity which, as far as I have observed, has become, strangely in a time of forced separation, much more of an expression of church being family, and a gaining of things that there will not be the desire to lose as things move forward to a new normal. I heard a leader of one historic denomination say,

"Will we want to go back to the same patterns that we have used for long enough?"

2. DOES CHURCH LOOK LIKE FAMILY?

CHURCHES OLD AND NEW

There is a wide variety of churches of historic denominations and non-denominations. Some of these keep more strictly to the patterns of life from previous generations, others have adapted and changed some of their lifestyle while maintaining their historic legacy, their ways of relating, and decision-making processes.

There have also arisen in the past generation many different "new" churches. Some of these are simply a congregation based in a community, others have grown into or joined with others to become a distinct grouping / network/ stream/ denomination, having a shared identity and organisation. There are also new congregations which have been planted out of already existing churches which then continue the "parent" church's ways of expression.

My observation has been that some new churches, which started a generation ago with a distinctiveness and effectiveness which was very different from the "old" style of church, have continued to keep to their same pattern of service which was then new but is now old. Others have even gone back from having services based on congregational involvement to become more liturgical and "led from the front", much more like the church style that they were once distinct from.

In old and new churches, there are experiments with different expressions of church life – some replacing traditional services with something completely different, some seeking to blend a mixture of old and new, traditional and contemporary, some dividing off age groups to have youth church, or children's church, some thereby making room for "adult church" to be undisturbed by the needs/ aspirations/ expressions of youth and children!,

4

some moving from a traditional base to "emerging church", some providing café church, some the family-friendly "Messy Church".

THE MEETING PLACE

I am particularly interested in the way that a meeting place is set up for the intended purpose, and whether the place, the positioning of furniture, people and decoration helps or hinders or restricts the fulfilment of the gathering's purpose.

The effect of these things is obvious when we think of how we decorate and position things in the various rooms of our own home, and especially how we tidy up, adjust, remove or add things when we are welcoming visitors; how we make the space fit the purpose of our being together.

I perhaps began to have sensitivity to this in a church setting many years ago when I was helping a Bible teacher set up the building for his talk which he did standing at a table with a reading desk. He asked me to set out a front row of chairs closer than normal to the place where he would be standing. This is because he knew that no one would want to sit on the front row, but when they sat on the second row, they would be where he would want the first row of his hearers to be!

I think that we can be so familiar with the places we meet and how they are configured, and what we do there by habit, that we can be unaware of what they suggest about the nature of church.

FIRST IMPRESSIONS

If our understanding of what church is was informed only by a attending a church service, what conclusions might we reach by how things are set up and what is done?

Entering a traditional Anglican or Roman Catholic church, we may have the perception that church means coming into a religious ritual, consisting of a number of actions performed according to a prescribed order, with a set way of approaching and responding to God.

Entering a traditional Presbyterian or free church might give the impression that church means coming to hear God's Word being preached for us to go and obey.

Entering a "traditional" new church setting might suggest that church is a cross between a music concert and a teaching conference.

Enter churches of any of the above and you may find that church looks like an educational institution, where ages are divided in parallel to schooling.

The altar, and the pulpit, the worship band, the separate age groups and all that goes with them are all in their different settings saying something of the intended purpose of the meeting.

Another aspect of what churches look like is the way in which many are described by how they are "governed": – Episcopal - by bishops, Congregational – by the congregation, Presbyterian - by elders, and worth mentioning that being led by elders in a local church whose decision-making "leaders" are solely from within that congregation, looks very different to the Church of Scotland with its national legal system of extensive and detailed rules covering every aspect of process and decision making affecting every congregation.

There can be relevance and appropriateness for many of the activities that all sorts of our different churches participate in. However, do people when they step in feel that they are coming into a meeting of brothers and sisters with their Father – into, as it were, the family's "living room"?

3. CHURCH IS FAMILY – ADJUSTING OUR THINKING

There are descriptive pictures in the New testament of the church being a body (1Corinthians 12v27), a building (Ephesians 2v21,22), and the branches of a vine (John 15v5) but to say that "Church is Family" is not to give a *picture* of what church is like or how it functions. It is not enough to say "church is like a family" or "church should be like a family" or "church should be a family". As will be seen from the New Testament studies that follow, to say "Church is Family" is to state a fundamental reality. This carries with it the uncomfortable challenge that any relationship, structure or function in a church which is not compatible with church being family must be in some way faulty.

PAST EXPERIENCES

There are understandable difficulties that we can have with the concept of "church is family" which arise from our background experience of both church and family.

Anyone who has had a negative, hurtful or damaging experience of church life, whether of impurity, legalism, control, or abuse may not be attracted to the idea that church is family – they might feel, "My family does not behave in the way that the church has. Church is not at all like family."

Some may interpret the statement in relation to a particular family type which they have experienced, whether insular, dysfunctional, broken, violent, temporary, complicated by children having different fathers, or domineered by a parent. They might properly feel, "I wouldn't want church to behave in the way my family has."

I remember being puzzled and surprised by the negative reaction I received from a very experienced and spiritual friend when I made the statement "Church is Family." From what I knew of her, I was sure that the concept would be attractive and meaningful to her – but it transpired that some aspects of her past experience of "family" was such that she did not want church to be like that.

CHURCH - ASSUMED NORMALITY

While we may not be affected by such negative associations with "church" and "family", we are likely to have a pre-set definition in our thought processes of what these words mean, arising from the particular and personal experience we have had of both.

If we have been part of a number of different styles of church, we may have a broader view of what "church" includes. If our experience has been limited to one church or churches in the same denomination/grouping, then we are likely to have a narrower concept of what "church" means which we will tend to apply to the statement "church is family".

From the time when I was sixteen years old, I knew that the focus of my life's work was to be in Christian ministry. Because at that time I was a member of a Baptist church, I assumed that such a call meant that I would be a Baptist minister, serving a local congregation which would probably be similar to Buckie Baptist Church where I was a member, so I would have expected to take two services on a Sunday and have an active young people's fellowship and for the church to be in Scotland. I have no recollection about whether at that time I expected to wear a minister's "dog collar" as part of my calling as my minister then did!

That was my pre-set concept of "church" which gave the boundaries to my thinking, so if at that time I had been presented with the statement, "Church is Family", I would have tried to fit "family" within these boundaries rather than thinking about how to perhaps radically change my thinking of "church" to make it fit with "Church is Family".

My subsequent years of ministry meant that the assumed normality of sixteen year old Graeme had to undergo drastic change, in my understanding of church and my place in it.

FAMILY - ASSUMED NORMALITY

Every family is different and each person in a family has their own distinct experience of what "family" means to them. If we each form our view of what "church is family" means based on our individual background, we may well come to very diverse conclusions about how it should (or should not) be expressed.

It will help us if we can recognise how our pre-set thinking concerning "family" might affect us in relating to church as "family".

"Church is family" does not mean that church has to be like my family or your family.

I have talked and prayed with many people over the years concerning how our experience in our own family, particularly our relationship with our father can affect how we view and relate to our heavenly Father and our place in church family. When doing this, I have always felt blessed that all my memories of my dad and our relationship were positive ones (except for the first time he took me for a haircut at a barber's!), and there was nothing that might hinder my relationship with my heavenly Father. Then one day, when I was thinking about him, a slightly different picture emerged. My dad was away in the Royal Navy for the first three years of my life, then we enjoyed some years of happy family life together, but he died as the result of an accident at work shortly before my seventh birthday. I asked myself the question, "How might I have been affected by that?" and it came to me that my resultant view of "father" might be of someone I looked up to and was loved by, but who was for most of the time "absent", and I can remember having to adjust my thinking to make sure that I did not believe or feel that about my heavenly Father.

So, before considering "Church is Family" in the Bible, what does the word "church" mean? and how might we describe the ingredients of perfect family?

4. THE WORD "CHURCH" IN THE BIBLE

The word church is used to translate the New Testament Greek word, *ekklesia*. *Ekklesia* comes from the word *ek* meaning "out" and *klesis* meaning "calling" .

It is used in the Bible to describe different types of assembly or gatherings of people.

In Acts 19v32, v41 it is used of a crowd (assembly) of people led by Demetrius a silversmith and other workmen with the same occupation who were stirred up about Paul's preaching.

In Acts 19v39 the town clerk instructed that any accusations should be taken to a lawful assembly – that is an authorised gathering of citizens to decide on issues.

In Acts 7v38 the word is used of the people of Israel in the desert.

So, in its simple meaning, it is a meeting or assembly of people – but rather than a random collection of people in the same place, it refers to a togetherness of purpose or identity which distinguishes them from others who are not in that grouping.

So in Acts 19v32 the people had been "called out" to demonstrate against Paul.

In Acts 19v39 the people would be "called out" to discuss and decide on issues.

In Acts 7v38 the people of Israel were "called out" from Egypt.

In the group of Christians I was with in Portessie in my childhood, and where I gave my life to Jesus, I didn't realise at that time the significance in the chosen description of "Assembly hall" for the building and "The Meeting" as the whole group identity – not just one particular service or get-together.

How the word church is used in the particular way that we think of it referring to Christians will be explored when we examine the Bible verses later.

5. FAMILY CHARACTERISTICS

Here are some characteristics of an ideal human family, so that we can have in our minds that if this is what "family" is meant to look like, then similar characteristics should be present in church life, and we can expect that this is expressed in what we find in the Bible.

PROVISION

When a baby is born into the family he/she is born into a place of loving security, provided with warmth (clothing), food, cleansing, comfort, and the nearness of others in being held/hugged/cuddled, and also the presence of others to interact with and be stimulated by sight, sound, touch, smell and taste. Their cries of distress are answered, their discomfort is soothed. They are given a place of rest.

At the beginning, nothing is required of them – everything is provided for them until as they develop they are gradually able to do things for themselves.

PROGRESSION

There is the expectation of development and help given to make progress without it being forced. Rather, delight is taken in each new step.

There is freedom for growth and self-expression and the encouragement to be who the child is, with distinct personality, gifts, talents, interests, skills.

PROTECTION

Family is a relationship which gives protection:
Protection from harm that may come from the actions of others.
Protection from harm that may come from the environment.
Protection from harm that may come from self.

PERMANANCE

When a child is born into a family, it cannot be unborn. There is a permanent relationship – and the parental relationship which defines the family is meant to be permanent too. There is a permanent acceptance of the child – they belong.

PARTICIPATION

There is a shared life in a family - a family home, with a responsibility towards one another, and an involvement in some way in the "family business" or calling, and a sharing in the fruits of the productivity of the family.

PURPOSE

A family and its family life can be a resource of blessing to others. Having been loved, there is the capacity to love; having been blessed, there is the resource to be a blessing.

6. BROTHERS AND SISTERS

While we are considering the meaning of words, it is important to note that in the New Testament, the word for brother is the same as the word for sister apart from the word ending:

brother - *ADELPHOS* (masculine word ending)

sister - *ADELPHE* (feminine word ending)

The word comes from the word *DELPHUS* which means womb, so signifies those from the same womb, or of the same origin.

So in the many places that the term "brothers" – *ADELPHOI* is used in addressing and describing followers of Jesus, it can include women together with men.

Some modern versions of the Bible reflect this by including "and sisters" in places where brothers are mentioned, where clearly it refers to the company of men and women.

At times the term *ANDRES ADELPHOI* meaning "Men brothers" is used to designate when speaking primarily to men, as when Stephen spoke to the Jewish council meeting in Acts 7v2.

CHURCH IS FAMILY
IN THE GOSPELS

To come to an understanding of Church is Family in the New Testament, we begin in the Gospels to look at what is described in:

1. The relationship of Father and Jesus.
2. The relationship of Father and disciples - not just the 12 apostles but the committed followers of Jesus.
3. The relationship of Jesus and followers.
4. The inter-relationships of Father, Jesus and followers.
5. The relationship of followers and one another.
6. How Jesus spoke to Father.

1. FATHER AND JESUS

1) FATHER'S SON

In Luke 1v35 Jesus is announced by the angel as one who will be called "God's son". Some Bible versions say he will be called "The Son of God", which sounds like a statement of his title or status. But in the Greek, there is not a "the" before son in this verse, so it reads "he will be called son of God" or as we would say, "God's son", which rather than conferring a title, is describing a "family" father/son relationship.

To mark Jesus out from others who will be called "God's children", Jesus is called in John 1v14 the "only-begotten *para Patros* from alongside Father".

"only -begotten" is the word usually used for an only child in a family – as the widow of Nain's son (Luke 7v12), Jairus' daughter (Luke 8v42), the demonized boy (Luke 9v38).

The relationship of *para* "from alongside" Father is described in John 1v18 as "the only-begotten who is in the bosom of the Father" picturing a close relationship of leaning right into him, as John did with Jesus when the nearest to him at the "last Supper" in John 13v23.

The preciousness of this relationship is demonstrated in John3v16 in that the extent of God's love for the world is seen in the giving of his only-begotten Son.

2) FATHER'S VOICE

There are two occasions in the Gospels where God speaks about Jesus in a voice that is audible to those present. First at his baptism (Matthew 3v17, Mark 1v11, Luke 3v22) and then when Jesus' appearance was changed on the mountain during his conversation with Moses and Elijah (Matthew 17v5, Mark 9v7, Luke 9v35). Of all the things that it is important to know about Jesus, the one thing that was spoken in this way is that Jesus is to his Father, "my loved Son in whom I am well pleased".

The first occasion marked him out as distinct from all the others who were being baptised, and the second marked him out from the Old Testament leaders, Moses and Elijah.

3) FATHER'S SON QUESTIONED

The Father and Son relationship was the fundamental issue about Jesus which was opposed and questioned:

- Satan's temptations of Jesus were "if you are God's Son..." (Luke 4v3,9)

- "The Jews tried all the harder to kill him; ...he was even calling God his own Father..." (John 5v18)

- At Jesus' trial the high priest said, "Tell us whether you are the Son of God." (Matthew 26v63)

- People passing by the cross shouted, "If you are God's Son, come down from the cross." (Matthew 27v40)

- Then we have the statement of the centurion, "Truly this man was son of God." It is sometimes questioned because there is no "the" before son whether the centurion was recognising Jesus as "the Son of God" or was saying he was a son of God. We don't know, but what we can see is that whatever the centurion's concept of "God" was, he recognised Jesus as being in a father/son relationship with him, that his character came from his relationship with God. (Matthew 27v54)

4) JOHN WRITES OF THE FATHER / SON RELATIONSHIP.

John, when writing about Jesus preparing for his death says that Jesus knew that the time had come for him to leave this world and go to the Father (John 13v1). He continues that Jesus knew that the Father had given all things into his hands, and that he had come from God and was returning to God (John 13v3).

5) JESUS SPEAKS OF FATHER

JESUS SPEAKS OF FATHER WHEN DESCRIBING HIS FAMILY RELATIONSHIP WITH HIM

Jesus says that His Father has held nothing back from him. He knows the Father in a way that no one else does, except when he reveals Father to them (Matthew 11v27). He does not act independently, but in relationship with his loving Father, he carries out what he sees Father wants done. (John 5v19,20)

JESUS SPEAKS OF FATHER WHEN SPEAKING ABOUT GOD IN HIS TEACHING

When his disciples told Jesus that some Pharisees were offended at his teaching, he described them as plants that "my heavenly Father has not planted" which would be pulled up. (Matthew 15v13)

When Simon Peter made his statement that Jesus was the Christ, the Son of the living God, Jesus attributed that revelation to God by saying that it did not come to Peter from a human agency, but from "My Father in heaven."(Matthew 16v17)

JESUS SPEAKS OF FATHER WHEN SAYING WHY HE WAS DOING WHAT HE WAS DOING

The first words recorded for us that Jesus said are about his relationship with God, and he uses the phrase, "my Father". When he was found in the temple by his mother, he said, "Did you not know that I must be in the things of my Father?"(*literal translation*) (Luke 2v49). His mother had just said to him, "Your father (meaning Joseph) and I have been anxiously searching for you." While Joseph was legally his father, yet at 12 years old Jesus was aware of his own family identity as God's Son.

Jesus said that all his actions were linked with what the Father was doing (John 5v19). What Jesus said, and the way he spoke were in response to what his Father wanted (John 12v49). His love for his Father led him to do exactly what his Father instructed him to do (John 14v31).

JESUS SPEAKS ABOUT FATHER IN DISCUSSIONS ABOUT WHO HE WAS

The most infuriating thing about Jesus for his opponents was the Father/Son relationship he spoke of, and was ultimately why they wanted him killed.

- When challenged about healing a man on the Sabbath, Jesus said that because his Father was always at work, so was he. The Jews wanted to kill him because Jesus calling God his Father was making himself equal with Him (John 15v17,18).

- When Jesus spoke about coming down from heaven, he said that the Father would give eternal life to those who looked to and believed in the Son, and the Jews questioned how he could say these things when they knew who his family were (John 6v40-42).

- When Pharisees did not believe what Jesus was saying about himself, he said that his Father would say the same about himself as he was saying (John 8v18,19) and that his Father was the One that they claimed as their God (John 8v34).

- In conversation with Jews who were asking him whether he was the Messiah, Jesus said, "I and the Father are One", and this resulted in them picking up stones to throw at him because they saw this as blasphemy, "because you, a mere man, claim to be God"(John 10v30-33).

2. FATHER AND FOLLOWERS

1) FAMILY LIFESTYLE

It seems that without any introduction or explanation, Jesus begins to talk to his followers as those who have a relationship with God as their Father.

JESUS ENCOURAGES THEM TO HAVE A LIFESTYLE THAT IS COMPATIBLE WITH THAT RELATIONSHIP.

He says that their lifestyle of good works should be so distinctive that people will see that it comes from their Father in heaven (Matthew 5v16).

He expects them, in line with being sons of their Father in heaven, to love their enemies and pray for those who persecute them (Matthew 5v44), and to be merciful to others just as their Father is merciful (Luke 6v36).

2) FATHER'S COMMITMENT

JESUS TELLS THEM OF THEIR FATHER'S COMMITMENT TO THEM.

He says that Father is committed to rewarding them for their service done to bless others or in devotion to Him that no one else is aware of (Matthew 6v4,6).

They can be confident that their Father knows what they need before they ask Him (Matthew 6v8). They don't need to worry about the essential things of life, because if they seek His kingdom, He will give them all they need. And more than that, their Father is happy for them to enjoy all that is in His kingdom (Luke 12v22,30-32).

3) TALKING TO FATHER

JESUS TELLS THEM HOW TO TALK TO FATHER.

When the disciples ask for instruction in prayer, Jesus does not introduce them to a religious ritual in order to approach a distant Creator, but tells them to take their place in the family and say simply, "Our Father" (Luke 11v2). We are so used to that phrase in the context of the often recited "Lord's Prayer" that its significance can be missed. He was saying that they/we can talk to God/Father the same way that He did. We are in the family.

4) FAMILY RELATIONSHIP

JESUS EMPHASISES THE IMPORTANCE OF THAT RELATIONSHIP.

He says that name of "Father" is to be honoured: "May your name be kept holy" (Luke 11v2). The word "name" conveys the whole character of a person, so that the description of them is always accurate. And what is the name that Jesus has given of God to his followers? "Our Father".

He says that no other relationship should interfere with, or in any way take the place of that special place we have with Father. He said not to call anyone on earth "father" because we have a Father in heaven (Matthew 23v9).

This statement could be misinterpreted if it is taken out of context.

When Jesus said to call no one on earth "father", he was not saying that we should disregard our **family** heritage. In Mark

7v9-13 Jesus rebukes the Pharisees and teachers of the law for disregarding their parents.

When Jesus said to call no one on earth "father", he was not saying that we should disregard our **ancestral** heritage. In Acts 7v2 Stephen speaks of "the God of glory appeared to our father, Abraham" and in Romans 4v1 Paul refers to Abraham as "our forefather according to the flesh", that is the Jewish people's human ancestor.

When Jesus said to call no one on earth "father", he was not saying that we should disregard our **spiritual** heritage. In Romans 4v16, Paul speaks of Abraham as the father of us all – that is - Abraham trusted in God, and all those who do likewise are in the same family.

When Jesus said, "Call no one on earth father", he was contrasting his way with that of the religious Pharisees who thrived on recognition by others of their perceived special status. "They love to be greeted in the market places and to have men call them 'Rabbi' (Teacher)" (Matthew 23v7). Jesus instructs his followers to neither accept or seek titles such as "Teacher", and not to give such titles as "Father" to anyone which would suggest that they have a superior status to others. Jesus' followers were all to be brothers and sisters with one another and to seek to serve rather than to be served.

Of course, Jesus was also pointing out that if we have the real thing, we don't need a substitute. We don't need to look to anyone else to fulfil the place of a father in our lives when we have the best and truest father – our Father in heaven, to whom we have direct access.

Did Paul break the rule?

In 1 Corinthians 4v14, Paul writes to those he describes as his dear children, saying that although they may have many instructors, they don't have many fathers – only himself who fathered them by the Gospel.

Paul is pointing to a special relationship he had with the Corinthians, as it was through what Paul said and did that they came to put their faith in Jesus. But he is not seeking a superior status to them. On the contrary, the letter is written to correct those who had been disregarding what Jesus had instructed, and were describing themselves as followers of Paul, or Apollos or Peter(1 Corinthians 1v11-13). Paul rebukes them for putting himself and those others in such a position, and instead says that they are "only servants" doing what God had given them to do, through whom the Corinthians came to believe (1 Corinthians 3v5).

5) FATHER'S CHILDREN

WHY ARE JESUS' FOLLOWERS ABLE TO RELATE TO GOD AS THEIR FATHER?

John 1v12 says that to all who received him (Jesus), who believed in his name, he gave the right to become God's children – born not in the normal way, but born of God.

3. JESUS AND HIS FOLLOWERS

We have seen how Jesus spoke of his own relationship with Father, and also how he expected his followers to relate to God as their Father, so now we look at what Jesus said about the relationship of his followers to himself.

1) FAMILY RELATIONSHIP

In Mark 3v31-35 there is the account of Jesus' mother and brothers coming to see him. They did not understand about his ministry and they came to take him away as they thought he had gone out of his mind. Being unable to get near him because of the crowd, they sent a message that they would like to talk with him, and no doubt the crowd would have expected Jesus to give priority to his family's request.

Instead he stays where he is and points to those who are responding positively to his teaching and describes such followers as , "my brother, my sister, my mother."

2) FAMILY PRIVILEGE

In Matthew 17v24-27, the question was put as to whether Jesus paid the religious tax which was the requirement made by Moses (Exodus 30v11-16) for everyone 20 years old and above. Peter hastily answered that he did, but Jesus had more to say to Peter on the matter. He asked Peter who earthly kings took custom or tribute from, their own sons, or others? When Peter said "others." Jesus said to him, then "the sons are free."(from having to pay). Jesus is saying that "sons" (of God) are free from the obligation to pay this tax to "their father".

We can easily see that because of who he is, Jesus was exempted from the obligation to give, but the amazing thing here is that he puts Peter in the same family relationship as himself. "then are the sons free". Jesus did not say, "Well, Peter, you should pay the tax like everyone else, but I don't need to..." Instead he says. "Lest we offend them..." and instructs Peter to take a miraculously placed coin from the mouth of a fish and give it – not just for himself but for "me and you" – both of them sons who were "free".

3) FAMILY COMMITMENT

In Matthew 25v40, when speaking about caring for people in need, Jesus said, " In whatever ways you have done it to one of the least of these my brothers, you have done it to me."

Jesus does not elaborate on who might be described as "the least of these my brothers", but he is expressing a family commitment to them in saying that he will take what is done to them as having been done to himself and deal with it accordingly.

4) FAMILY GET-TOGETHER

At Jesus' tomb in Matthew 28, the two Marys were told by an angel to go quickly and tell his disciples that he is risen from the dead, and that they would see him in Galilee. (v7)

Before they passed on that message, Jesus himself appeared to the women to change the message. He said "Go tell <u>my brothers</u>" (v10). It was not a change of who the message was for, but a change of name.

And following that we read that (v16) <u>the disciples</u> went to Galilee and saw Jesus there.

So after their failure to stand by Jesus at his time of trial, the disciples were being reassured of their place in the family as Jesus' brothers.

5) FAMILY BUSINESS

In John 15v15 Jesus says to his disciples that he would no longer call them servants because servants don't know their master's business. Instead he calls them friends because he has made known to them everything he has heard from his Father.

This is not in opposition to his speaking of them as his brothers in Father's family, but instead it is describing how they would work together for God's Kingdom. In the family business, they were being taken from the shop floor to the boardroom. That did not change their place in the family.

There is more about Jesus' relationship with his followers which we shall see when we look at what is said about the inter-relationship of Father, Jesus and Followers.

4. THE INTER-RELATIONSHIPS OF FATHER, JESUS AND FOLLOWERS

1) JESUS MAKES FATHER KNOWN TO HIS FOLLOWERS

In Matthew 11, when John the Baptist is asking questions about Jesus' identity, and others are describing him as a glutton who drank too much and kept the wrong sort of company, Jesus says that Father makes things clear to those who were humbly following Jesus (v25) and that he, Jesus, makes Father known to those who come to him and learn from being alongside him in his gentleness and humility (v27-30).

The family outcome of this is described in John 1v12 where all who receive Jesus are given the right to become God's children.

2) JESUS' FATHER IS HIS FOLLOWERS' FATHER

In Matthew 18 Jesus speaks to his followers about the place of children in the kingdom of heaven. In referring to their preciousness, he says, "Don't despise one of these little ones. For I tell you that their angels in heaven always look on the face of **my** father in heaven" (v10), and continuing on the same subject he says "**your** father in heaven does not want any of these little ones to be lost." (v14)

3) FATHER IN JESUS, JESUS IN FOLLOWERS

In John 14, When Philip asked Jesus to show them the Father (v8), Jesus answered by saying that he who had seen him (Jesus) had seen the Father (v9) and that "I am in the Father and the Father in me" (v10).

We are familiar with what someone might say of a boy, "Oh, I can see his father in him", meaning that the way he looks or sounds or acts is like his father. Jesus describes what it means that he is in the Father and the Father in him by saying that the words he speaks are not just his own but are from relationship with Father, and that the things that he does are by the Father "dwelling" in him.

That Father/Jesus relationship is obvious by the things that Jesus said and did, but Jesus then goes on to speak of his followers' experience as an extension of that quality and depth of relationship. He speaks of his followers doing ongoing works the same as his own, that he would work through them as his Father worked though him, that the Holy Spirit would be given to them and that they would come to know that "I am in the Father, and you in me, and I in you." (v20) – so that they would not be saying things from their own initiative, but from him, and that he would work through their actions.

Little words can convey much – and the word "in" is massive in meaning about the inter-relationship of Father, Jesus and us.

Father in Jesus – Jesus in Father – us in Jesus – Jesus in us.

This profound truth is couched in homely family terms by Jesus in the chapter:

The noun "*mone*" an abode, dwelling place (home) and the verb "*meno*" – to stay, abide, dwell are used:

- In my Father's house are many dwellings (v2)
- The Father that dwells in me (v10)
- I shall give you another called alongside to dwell with you for ever (v16)
- You know him (The Holy Spirit) because he dwells beside you and shall be in you (v17)
- If anyone loves me, they will keep my words, and my Father will love them and we will make our dwelling beside them. (v23)

We are meant to be as much at home with Jesus as Jesus is with his Father.

This inter-relationship of Father, Jesus and followers means that from the relationship that Jesus has with Father come the things that Jesus says and does, and from the relationship that followers have with Jesus come the things that they say and do. That is both an astonishing promise, and a massive challenge to live in the reality of Jesus' words.

4) ONENESS OF FATHER, JESUS AND FOLLOWERS

In John 17v20,21 Jesus makes it clear that the relationship about the oneness of his followers he is talking about is not just for the 12 disciples – but for all his followers, "that they all may be one".

This prayer of Jesus is often portrayed as Jesus praying that his followers will all agree with one another in their relationship of followers to followers, for example in seeking a unanimous decision at a church meeting, or the willingness of churches of different denominations to work together, or Christians joining together in some prayer project.

What Jesus is praying for is even more profound than any of those, however desirable they are.

Rather , it is the oneness of

- Father being in Jesus

- Jesus being in Father

- Followers being in Jesus and Father,

so that just as the life of Jesus demonstrated his relationship (oneness) with Father, so followers' lives would demonstrate their relationship (oneness) with Jesus.

The glory that Jesus had of Father in him, and him in Father, is extended to his followers – Father in Jesus and Jesus in followers – that oneness of relationship with Jesus in which we experience the love of Father as Jesus experienced it. (v22,23)

5) FATHER'S LOVE FOR JESUS' FOLLOWERS

In John 16v23-27 Jesus tells his followers of the special privilege they have in their relationship with Father. Jesus' disciples were used to experiencing what Jesus received from Father and then passed on to them, but with Jesus about to leave them, the issue arose of how they should now relate to receiving from Father. Jesus speaks of them asking and receiving from Father "in my name" – that is, because of Jesus and their relationship with him, they could ask and receive from Father. "My Father will give you whatever you ask in my name" (v23).

But Jesus wants them to be clear that his special standing in relation to Father is not a barrier between them and Father, so that they have to ask Jesus, and Jesus will then ask Father. Rather, Jesus' special standing and their relationship with him means that they have direct access to talk to Father who loves them. "In that day, you will ask in my name. I am not saying that I will ask the Father on your behalf. No, the Father himself loves you because you have loved me, and believed that I came from alongside God."(v26)

The word here translated "love" is the word *phileo*. It is a word which speaks of friendship. There is not just one English word that would fit as a translation of all the times *phileo* is used in the New Testament. A range of expressions that could be used are: The Father is fond of you, is affectionate towards you, is your friend, has a father's love for you.

The word is used a number of times about family relationships: *philadelphos* – loving brothers and sisters (1 Peter 3v8), *philandros* – loving of one's husband (Titus 2v4), *philoteknos* – loving one's children (Titus 2v4); so here, when speaking of Father, it is about his affectionate fatherly relationship with His family, and his family's relationship with Jesus.

The word *phileo* is the word used in some places translated "to kiss", so we might picture that Father's attitude to us is of open arms to welcome and receive us with a hug.

While this is not an exact translation, I think that Jesus is wanting them to know: "Your Dad likes you, so there is no reason why you should be afraid to come to him and bring him all you need to ask Him about." I think that this revelation by Jesus demolishes much of what is done in organised religion!

6) FOLLOWERS OF JESUS, CHILDREN OF FATHER

When Jesus appeared to Mary Magdalene on the day of his resurrection, he had a message for his disciples. He did not mention their weakness, their failure, their not standing with him in the time leading up to his death. They might well have been wondering about themselves and how their relationship with God would be affected.

But Jesus' message is an overwhelmingly encouraging one for them. In John 20v17, he says, "Go and tell <u>my brothers.</u>" When Mary told them, they knew that Jesus still considered them as his brothers, and then he says, " I am ascending to <u>my</u> Father and <u>your</u> Father, and to <u>my</u> God and <u>your</u> God." This is a summary of the completed work of Jesus: that the way has been opened up for us to be accepted by Jesus as his brothers and sisters, and accepted by Father as His children.

7) FOLLOWERS AS FAMILY OF FATHER, JESUS AND THE HOLY SPIRIT

In Matthew 28v19 Jesus links those who are becoming disciples with Father and Son and the Holy Spirit. However most English translations do not convey the exact meaning when they say, "baptising them in the name of the Father and the Son and the Holy Spirit."

To clarify this, we need to look at a number of Greek words, what they each mean and how they are used in the New Testament. When the phrase "in the name of" is used in English translations, there are three words that are translated as "in".

- There is the word *en* which means "in", so when we see the phrase where *en* occurs "in the name of" we understand it as "on the authority of".

In John 5v43 Jesus says, "I have come in (*en*) my Father's name and you do not accept me; but if someone else comes in (*en*) his own name, you will accept him."

- There is the word "*epi*" which means "upon" so when we see the phrase where "*epi*" is translated "in the name of", it means "on the foundation or basis of that name", using that name (rightly or wrongly) as the basis for what is being done.

In Luke 21v8 Jesus says, "Many will come in (*epi*) my name.." He does not mean that they are coming on his authority, but that they are using his name (wrongly) as the basis for what they are saying.

In Acts 4v17,18, 5v28,40 The apostles were ordered to stop speaking and teaching "in (*epi*) the name of Jesus". This did not mean to stop acting on Jesus' authority, to stop doing what Jesus was telling them to do, but to stop using the name of Jesus as the basis and justification for their teaching.

- There is the word "*eis*" which means "into", so when we see the phrase "*eis*" in "in the name of " it does not mean on his authority, but recognising, or taking on, being included in the identity of that name, that person.

In Matthew 28v19 the phrase should more accurately read "baptising them into (*eis*) the name of the Father, the Son and the Holy Spirit". So while baptising people is done on the authority of Jesus, that is not what is being said here. It signifies that when a person is baptised they are recognising, and being accepted into the identity of that named person, so being accepted into the identity of the Father, the Son and the Holy Spirit – so being accepted into God's family.

John 1v12 says: "To as many as received him (Jesus), to them he gave the authority to become God's children – those who believed into (*eis*) his name."

In Acts 19v3 Paul asked a group, not "on what authority were you baptised?", but "Into (eis) what were you baptised, and they replied, "Into (*eis*) John's baptism". Then when they heard what Paul said, v5 "they were baptised into (*eis*) the name of the Lord Jesus."

In 1 Corinthians 1, Paul addresses the issue of people in the church defining themselves by identifying with a particular name – some saying, "I am of Paul, others, I am of Apollos, others I am of Cephas" (v12) Paul responded by saying: "Is Christ divided? Was Paul crucified for you? or were you baptised into (*eis*) the name of Paul?"(v13)

So being baptised into the name of the Father, the Son, and the Holy Spirit is being accepted into God's family with his family name as ours – with Father as our father, and being named with Jesus – Christ-ians.

This might be pictured in the way that when a child is adopted into a family, their name is sometimes changed to the family name of their new family to recognise their new identity – so "adopted into the name of the family"; or while it is not always done, when a couple are married it is common for the wife to change her surname to be "married into the name of her husband".

So baptism shows the family to which we belong – the family of Father, Son and Holy Spirit. We can link this back to Jesus' baptism where Father acknowledges Jesus as his Son, acknowledging his family relationship.

5. FOLLOWERS AND FOLLOWERS

Along with Jesus' general teaching to his followers, he gave some instructions about their relationships with one another as brothers and sisters in his family.

1) FAMILY PRAYERS

In Matthew 6v9 Jesus said, "After this manner, pray…" Jesus then taught them to pray using "Our Father" – thus indicating that in recognising God as their father, they are recognising one another as brothers and sisters, and they should relate to one another as such. Also in saying that they should say, "Our Father" he implies that they would be praying together with one another.

2) FAMILY DISPUTES

Things can go wrong in family relationships, and in Luke 17v3 and Matthew18v15-17, Jesus shows how such things can and should be addressed and put right.

These are <u>family</u> instructions – they do not apply in the same way in dealing with people outside the family.

If wronged by a fellow-follower – a brother – go on your own and tell him, and if he repents, forgive him. This makes clear the aim of confronting a wrong: it is not to condemn, or shame or make the person feel bad, or make them pay for what they have done, but for peace and fellowship to be restored. (Luke 17v3) "If he listens to you, you have won your brother." (Matthew 18v15).

If the issue cannot be resolved between the two of you, then the instruction is to take one or two others to get a clear picture of what has happened and help the issue to be resolved (v16). It is worth noting that Jesus simply says "one or two more", not particularly elders or leaders. This is not an organisational protocol, but rather a get-together of brothers to resolve a family dispute, with the hope and intention of helping the guilty one acknowledge their error.

Then if the person will not be corrected, then the matter should be made known to the "church" – the assembly – the gathered family *ekklesia* (v17).

This is the only time that Jesus uses this word *ekklesia* (literally: called out ones) apart from in Matthew 16v18 – "upon this rock I will build my church" *ekklesia*.

If the person is still unrepentant, they should be treated as someone who is not a member of the family. Of course this did not mean that they should no longer be shown love, as Jesus expected his followers to not only show respect to their fellow brothers and sisters, but to be distinctive in the way that they showed respect to those outside the family. Matthew 5v47 says, "If you greet (show respect to) only your brothers, what are you doing more than others do? Don't even the pagans do that?"

3) FAMILY CORRECTION

In Luke 6v41 Jesus asks, "Why do you look at the speck in your brother's eye?"

In family life we can easily get annoyed when a brother or sister does not "see things" in the way that we do, and Jesus gives instructions in the context of him having said in Luke 6v36,37 that his followers should be merciful forgiving and generous, not judgemental or condemning. Jesus warns his followers about getting concerned about small perceived faults in our brothers and sisters, while not giving proper attention to correcting major deficiencies in ourselves.

I grew up in a church culture where there was an emphasis on telling people, "You're wrong!" and seeking to correct them from any deviation from what was considered to be the acceptable path of Christian doctrine or behaviour. The way that this was sometimes done, with little thought about the pain that might be caused in the process, suggests that there may have been undealt with planks in our eyes as we tried to remove our brother's speck!

Notice that Jesus does not say that we should be unconcerned about something that is preventing our brother or sister to "see clearly", or about what gets in our way – but that we should give our attention to what hinders us, so that we can have clear, loving and accurate judgement and insight into what can help our brother or sister.

I have found that the Holy Spirit only ever raises an issue to be dealt with when it is the right time and context where it can be healed or put right without the person suffering hurt or damage in the process. We should be careful to address any perceived issues in one another in a way that accords with that.

4) FAMILY EQUALITY

In Matthew 23v8 Jesus says, "All you are brothers". In these few words, Jesus sums up the essence of the relationship of his followers to one another. No one is less than a brother or sister; no one is more than a brother or sister. This is so important that it merits some detailed attention.

First let us look at the context in which Jesus says these words:

In Matthew 23v1-7 Jesus, when speaking of people who claim they are seeking to disciple others in the ways of God – the teachers of the Law and the strict rule-keeping Pharisees – he describes them as looking for recognition, privilege, honour socially, religiously and by the community. They see themselves as those who are in some way set apart from ordinary people in their devotion, and look to be recognised as "Rabbis" – teachers and guides who have a following of disciples of their ways of thinking and doing things. Jesus' followers are not to be like them!

The term, "Rabbi" – (my master / my teacher) is not to be used by them.

Jesus' followers are to teach others and to make disciples – but not disciples or followers of themselves but of Jesus.

Notice that Jesus does not just say, "Do not <u>want</u> to be called, "Rabbi", or, "Do not <u>seek</u> to be called Rabbi", but rather, "Do not <u>be</u> <u>called</u> Rabbi." – Do not accept such a designation from other followers of Jesus, and do not have that kind of relationship which separates you from them in status.

You are all brothers and sisters – the only one who is different is "Rabbi, Jesus" – (our Master / our Teacher/ our Guide)

This title "Rabbi" was used of Jesus

- by those interested in hearing him.

Two disciples of John the Baptist asking Jesus, "Rabbi, where do you live?" (John 1v38)

Nicodemus: "Rabbi, we know that you are a teacher who has come from God." (John 3v2)

- and by his committed followers:

Peter said to Jesus, "Rabbi, it is good for us to be here." (Mark 9v5)

His disciples asked, "Rabbi, who sinned, this man or his parents that he was born blind?" (John 9v2)

- It was also used by Judas Iscariot to identify Jesus to those who had come to arrest him:

Going at once to Jesus, Judas said, "Rabbi!" and kissed him. The men seized Jesus and arrested him. (Mark 14v45,46)

While the word, "Rabbi" is not used by Christians of one another, in many churches and denominations, designations are used of some people which may give the impression of a similar distinction of status with the expectation that they will be treated in a different way from other "brothers and sisters".

Terms like clergy, priest, reverend, and even pastor can move from being a description of a person's work and responsibility to being a designation that sets him or her apart from the rest of "the congregation".

Whatever titles people may have been given because of historical / denominational practices, they are in Jesus' family no less and no more than a brother or sister, due no less and no more honour and respect than any other.

5) FAMILY ENCOURAGEMENT

In Luke 22v32 Jesus said to Simon Peter, "When you are turned, strengthen your brothers."

This simple little statement is a great source of encouragement to followers of Jesus.

Simon Peter is about to face his own failure to live up to the strong words of commitment he has said about him following Jesus.

When Jesus said, "When you are turned.." it means that failure is not to be final – there is a way back. When Jesus says, "Strengthen your brothers" , he is indicating to Simon Peter that he will still be a "brother" – his failure will not mean that he will lose his place in the family. His failure does not mean that he can no longer have a place of service – he is to strengthen others – and he is to remember that the "others" he is strengthening are his "brothers" and so in his relationship to them he is to treat them as such – he is their brother.

We will see in Acts how Peter lives this out, but it is worth mentioning here that what Jesus said to him stayed with him, as can be seen from his letter: "Therefore, my <u>brothers</u>...."(2 Peter 1v10) "I will not be negligent to put you always in remembrance of these things, though you know them, and are <u>strengthened</u> in the truth you have." (v12)

6) FAMILY RELATIONSHIP

In John 21v23 we read, "the rumour spread among the brothers..." Jesus' description of his followers as brothers and sisters of one another is picked up here by the writer when describing the "family rumour" that the disciple, John would still be alive when Jesus returned. He uses the term which we will find is the common one elsewhere in the New Testament of Christians' relationship with one another – the saying went among "<u>the brothers</u>". In not defining this word, the writer shows that it was commonly understood and used by those to whom he was writing.

6. JESUS SPEAKING TO FATHER

Jesus taught his followers to know his Father as their father, and when they pray to say, "Our Father". It is instructive to see how Jesus related to his Father in talking with him, as an example for us, his followers and family.

1) EXPRESSION OF JOY

Matthew 11v25-27; Luke 10v21

Matthew gives, before this prayer, the general negative background of rejection which Jesus had faced in some places despite the miracles he had performed. Luke gives us the immediate context of the return of those whom Jesus had sent out on mission and who had seen a good response, and victories over evil.

Jesus begins, "Father, Lord of heaven and the earth." and Luke describes this as an outburst of Holy Spirit joy. Rather than an expression of thanks or praise (as in some translations) the word used by Jesus to describe his statement (*exomologoumai*) means an open declaration. So while it is addressed to his Father, it is meant for all around to hear, and to know how Jesus feels.

My loose paraphrase would be: "Father, you are above everyone and everything everywhere, and I want everyone to know that I am very glad that even though there are people who have had all the evidence they need and who still reject what we are saying and doing, you have helped these ordinary people that I have sent out on a Kingdom mission to grasp what we are about and to put it into practice – with the result that you have brought other ordinary folk into the good of it. You are well-pleased with that plan – and so am I."

Jesus' example reminds us that "Our Father" is also "Lord of heaven and the earth". Negative responses in some situations do not mean that Father's plan is not working. We can expect ordinary people with no background learning to be open to and receive revelation from Father. The word Jesus uses when he says "you have revealed to babes" is *nepios* which means a "non-speaker", so while here Jesus is using the word figuratively, it also applies literally: "Out of the mouths of babes and sucklings, you have ordained praise/strength" (Psalm 8v2, Matthew 21v16)

2) EXPRESSION OF CONFIDENCE

John 11v41

Jesus said, "Father, I thank you that you have heard me…. I said this for the benefit of those listening." – This is when Lazarus is about to be raised back to life.

There are occasions recorded of Jesus talking to his Father where we do not know the content of their conversation: At Jesus' baptism (Luke 3v21); Before a mission journey (Mark 1v35); Before appointing the 12 apostles (Luke 6v12); After dealing with large crowds (Matthew 14v23, Mark 6v46, Luke 5v16); Before talking to his disciples about the sufferings he would face (Luke 9v18); On the mountain where Peter, James and John saw him transfigured (Luke 9v28).

It is clear that we are meant to learn from his habit and lifestyle of prayer, but also specifically from those occasions when he allowed his talking to Father to be overheard by those who were with him. So here, the situation is at the tomb of Lazarus, and Jesus is thanking Father for hearing what he wants in this situation, and for always hearing him.

This thank-you prayer is spoken out so that the people around will hear it. Jesus is about to call for dead Lazarus to be raised back to life. He wants this to be attributed to his relationship with Father. It connects with what Jesus said, "Let your light shine among people that they may see your good works <u>and glorify your Father in heaven</u>."(Matthew 5v16)

Sometimes it is good for others to hear our expressions of thanks and gratefulness for what our relationship with Father brings to us. It is important sometimes for people to know that we are praying for their situation, so that when they receive an answer, they attribute it rightly to our Father.

3) EXPRESSION OF BEING TROUBLED

John 12v27

"Now my soul is troubled. What shall I say? Father save me from this hour? But it was for this reason I came to this hour. Father, glorify your name."

It is interesting how Jesus shows the "familiness" of prayer by stepping into talking with Father in the course of conversation with those who are with him.

In Luke 10v20 Jesus says to the people – "rejoice that your names are written in heaven" then "at that time, Jesus...said, "...Father, Lord of heaven and earth..." (v21)

In John 11v40 He says to Martha "Did I not tell you…" Then Jesus looked up and said, "Father, I thank you that you have heard me…" (v41)

Here in John 12v26 to the people Jesus says, "… my Father will honour the one who serves me" then he moves straight into thinking aloud, "Now my soul is troubled …. for this reason I came to this hour" then immediately into speaking to Father, "Father, glorify your name!"

Jesus has said in v23 that "The hour is come that the Son of Man should be glorified", then he speaks of a grain of wheat falling into the ground and dying, so in his teaching, he has brought to mind what he is about to face. The result was that, at that point, his mind and emotions were stirred in anticipation of the suffering. His immediate reaction was to bring his thoughts and feelings to Father, and he thinks out loud about what his request should be. He decides against asking to avoid the cost of the path he is on, in favour of seeking whatever will bring glory to Father.

There is a remarkable instant audible answer from heaven in agreement with his prayer, "I have glorified it and I will glorify it again." Jesus describes this as intended not for his benefit, but for those who had heard his prayer, and Father's answer.

Jesus' example encourages us, when our minds and emotions are troubled, not to be afraid of expressing that both to others and to Father. Whatever situation we face, we can bring it to Father. It is useful to think about what we really want, what we most want to ask for. Our view of what we would like for ourselves may not be the best in Father's plan, so it is good to consider, "What do I want, not for myself, but for Father in this situation?"

When we commit ourselves in seeking glory for Father, that in itself brings glory to Him – it allows others to see who He is as our Father, and what it is like to live in that relationship with Him – honouring Him above everything else.

4) EXPRESSION OF FAMILY CARE

John 17

Once again, Jesus, in the middle of a conversation with his disciples, moves straight into talking to Father. "Be of good cheer, I have overcome the world" Jesus spoke these words and lifted his eyes to heaven and said, "Father...."

This prayer is in the context of, and is about the implications of what I would call a time of family transition.

- Jesus had been with his family. "While I was with them..." (v12)

- He had been away physically from Father. "I have brought you glory on earth..." (v4)

- While in this setting he had introduced them to Father, and by their response to him, brought them into the family. "I gave them the words you gave me and they accepted them.." (v8)

- He had ensured their close relationship with Father while he was with them. "While I was with them I kept them in your name..." (v12)

- This was now the time of transition when he was about to leave the family and go to be with Father. "I will remain in the world no longer, but they are still in the world..." (v11) "And now I come to you..." (v13)

- He wants their relationship to be maintained and to be established strongly by Father. (v11) "Holy Father, keep them in your name.." (v13) and for the same to be true for all those who would later join the family. "Father, just as you are in me and I am in you may they also be in us..." (v21)

- Ultimately he wants his family to join him where he is with Father. "Father, I want those you have given me to be with me where I am..." (v24)

Jesus in his opening words draws attention to Father's family relationship – He does not say, "Father, glorify me", but, "Father, glorify your Son". Then later in the prayer he refers to Holy Father (v11)– drawing attention to His character, then later, Righteous Father (v25), drawing attention to His actions.

Looking at Jesus' prayer in John 17 with "family" in mind, I noticed his use of the phrase "your name" in verses 6,11,12,26. Some modern translations such as NIV, GNB and others give interpretations rather than translations of the phrase that Jesus used. In v6 and v26 they say "I have revealed you"; "I have made you known". While it is true that Jesus has done this, if he had wanted to convey that here, he could have chosen to say that, but it is not what he said. What he said was; "I have revealed your name" ; "I have made known your name".

In verses 11,12 where Jesus said "Keep them in your name"; "I kept them in your name", in these translations, Jesus' words are extended to "Protect them / keep them safe by the power of your name" "I have kept them by the power of your name". Once again, while there is truth conveyed in these words, they are not what Jesus said, and there are words he could have used to convey either the power or authority of God.

I can see a simpler and more consistent way of taking Jesus' words. While in other places in the Bible "name" can be used to signify a person, or their character/attributes, or their authority, it is perhaps easy to miss that it can also be saying simply the name of a person. While there are a number of different words that can be rightly used in speaking about God and relating to him, there is a name that Jesus revealed to his followers for their relationship with God: FATHER. As he had said to them, "When you pray, say, "Our Father.."

So what I see in these verses is Jesus conveying something like:

I have introduced them to you as their Father (v6); Holy Father, keep them in the relationship with you as their Father, which I have kept them in while I was with them (v11); I have made known to them what it means to have you as their Father, and I will continue to do that, so that the same love you have for me as your Son might be experienced by them as your children (v26).

In this prayer of Jesus, there are enough lessons to fill a whole book, but concentrating on Jesus' example to us in speaking to Father, here is my summary of what he said which we can learn from and put into practice:

You are my Father, and I am your Son. I have done, am doing and will continue to do all that you want me to do. I want all the blessing of joy, love, truth and glory that you have for me. I want for others in your family all the blessings of joy, truth, love and glory that you have for them. I want those who are not yet believers to come into all the blessings of joy, truth, love and glory that you have for them together with us. And ultimately for us all to be together with you.

5) EXPRESSION OF AGONY

Matt 26v36-46; Mark 14v32-42; Luke 22v39-46

Gethsemane

This is an awesome prayer to think about, and we will never know the depths and extent of the experience that Jesus went through at this time. Jesus had just had the special meal with the disciples and was about to deliberately put himself in the place where he could be found and arrested, knowing what would then happen to him. The full force of what he was facing came upon him. The words used to describe what was affecting him signify: to be sorrowful, crushed with anguish, depressed, dejected, grieved, distressed, in agony.

So what does he do? He takes it to Father – the father he knows as "Abba" – his local Aramaic dialect of the word that a child uses in addressing their own father.

Though what he is dealing with is intensely personal, he wants the company and support of his close friends, Peter, James and John, and he tells them what he is feeling (Mark 14v34), and he comes back to them twice looking for their fellowship with him.

This is no ordinary prayer-time. It is an overwhelmingly anguished time: he fell on his face and prayed (Matthew 26v39); he fell on the ground and prayed (Mark14v35); being in agony he prayed intensely and his sweat was like great drops of blood falling down to the ground (Luke 22v44).

The content of Jesus' conversation with Father is very simple in words but devastatingly far-reaching in its implications. The path of suffering that Jesus was already experiencing was, and would be, so painful that in anticipation of this he asks Father if he could be relieved of the responsibility of bearing it. He describes what he is facing as a cup (of suffering for sin) that his Father has given him. And here is the greatest and most costly decision ever made by Father and by His Son. It was Father's choice to give, and not to withdraw the cup. It was Jesus' choice to drink it. For even though three times Jesus asks his Father to take the cup away from him, he includes in his request the biggest "BUT" of history – "but not what I want – what you want."

Jesus' experience during this time of grappling with such immense issues was physically, mentally, emotionally and spiritually exhausting, and while Father's response was to not take the cup away from him, He did send an angel to strengthen him. And he was strengthened! Jesus got up from that prayer time and having no sleep that night, went forward to his arrest, trial suffering and death with a composure which would give no hint to those who were not there of what he had gone through in Gethsemane. He exhibited the "peace that passes understanding".

In the lesser but real challenges that we face, following Jesus' example we can remember when we come to God we come as children to our Father. When facing difficult situations it is good and right to ask for the support of others to be alongside us in prayer. There are times when others are facing a difficult situation when we can be faithful in standing with them to support them in prayer. It is alright to pray more than once about something – to keep asking until we are settled about the outcome. Jesus prayed three times and it says "using the same words" (Mark14v39). Whatever we feel that we need, it is good to include the "But" of faith – that leaves us open to Father's best choice. If Father, for his greater purposes does not want to take us out of a difficulty, He will give us strength to face going through it. Father chooses what He wants for us. He leaves it to us to choose whether to go with His choice.

6) EXPRESSION OF SELF-RESTRAINT

Matthew 26v53

To emphasise the deliberate choice that Jesus made about proceeding in the way that Father wanted, we have here the content of a request that Jesus could have made to Father but didn't.

"Do you think that even now I cannot call upon Father and he will give me more than 12 legions of angels?" A legion in the Roman army was 3000-6000 soldiers, so Jesus is talking about more than 72,000 angels being ready to act on his behalf if he required it. It is worth taking a minute to try to imagine what an army of 72,000 angels might look like, and to imagine what it would have looked like if he had made that request – and then to be very grateful that he did not!

There are always more than enough resources in heaven to act on our behalf if that is what we need. There are times when we could receive things from heaven, when it is better not to ask for them.

7) EXPRESSION OF FORGIVENESS

Luke 23v34

"Father, forgive them, they don't know what they are doing." The context of this prayer is Jesus being in the agony of having nails hammered through his hands and his feet to fix him to the cross.

Who are the "them" that Jesus is asking for forgiveness for here? And who were hearing what he said?

In one sense, everyone involved in any way with what led up to Jesus' crucifixion were doing something that they did not fully know or understand, but some of them knew what Jesus was like and deliberately wanted to get rid of him.

The timing of Jesus' prayer here focusses on those right there with him, the "they" of "When they had come to the place... there they crucified him. Then Jesus said, "Father, forgive them, they don't know what they are doing..." and they divided his clothes and cast lots. The "them" "they" were the group of soldiers who were hammering nails through his hands and his feet, fixing him to the cross. They were doing it without any real personal knowledge of Jesus. To them he was just another criminal and they were obeying orders, doing their job.

What must it have meant for these soldiers to hear these words? Jesus wanted them to hear them. The soldiers would have been used to others in the same situation crying out with anguish and fear, or anger and cursing at them, and here instead, they hear a prayer asking that they should be forgiven for what they were doing. I wonder if they ever asked, "What is it we did not know here?", "Why should he want to pray for us?", "What have we done that needs to be forgiven?"

Since we have this record of these words of Jesus to Father, either one of his followers was near enough to hear and take note of what he said, or one of the soldiers themselves reported what he said in praying for them.

Just at the point when we might have most expected Jesus to be seeking something from Father for himself, he is doing what he said his followers should do: "Pray for those who treat you badly" (Luke 6v28).

We should recognise that when some people offend us or treat us badly, they might not know what they are doing. When being ill-treated by others, is it ourselves or them that we are praying for?

Are we seeking their blessing? Jesus said that by loving our enemies and praying for those who persecute us, we show ourselves to be sons and daughters of our Father in heaven (Matthew 5v44).

Are we near enough to Jesus to hear what he is saying? Are we passing on his words of forgiveness to others?

It can be good and right sometimes to let people hear or know what we are praying for them, including people who would not be expecting us to be seeking blessing for them.

8) EXPRESSION OF ANGUISH AND FAITH

Matthew 27v46

About the ninth hour, Jesus cried out in a loud voice, *"Eloi, Eloi, lama sabachthani?"* which means, "My God, my God, why have you forsaken me?"

The context of this agonising prayer is that Jesus has been nailed to the cross, been mocked by people watching him, then there followed a period of three hours about which nothing is written except that darkness covered the whole land.

Then, Jesus has strength to cry out with a loud voice, and he cries in Aramaic, his local dialect. For the only time in the prayers of Jesus that are recorded for us, instead of addressing, "Father", he says, "My God" as he is quoting the words that begin Psalm 22.

It is very clear that along with expressing the terrible anguish of his suffering, these words are meant to direct us to Psalm 22 which goes on to describe prophetically some precise details of what Jesus was going through: e.g.

- "He trusted that the Lord would deliver him; let Him deliver him seeing as He delighted in him." (Psalm 22v8, Matthew 27v43).

- "They part my garments among them and cast lots for my clothes.". (Psalm 22v18, Matthew 27v35)

The psalm not only describes the suffering, but goes beyond that to a call for help and the outcome in Psalm 22v22-31

- "When he cried to Him he heard." (v24)

- "All the ends of the earth shall remember and turn to the Lord." (v27)

- and it contains the commitment, "I will declare your name to my brothers" (v22) which is what Jesus said in John 17v26: "I have made your name known to them, and I will continue to do so."

So Jesus' prayer is both an expression of utmost anguish yet also deepest faith. Whatever he is feeling at that point, he knows that it is part of God's perfect purpose, and it is not his last word! Jesus' prayer was also the heading of a Bible message for anyone there who recognised the words as being from Psalm 22 and went home to see what the rest of it said.

Words from the Bible can be a great help to us in times of distress – if we know them!

We can bring our "Why?" questions to Father. While never approaching in any way the intensity of what Jesus was suffering, there are times when we can feel that God is not with us in our time of distress and we don't understand why. There can be some known and some unknown reasons why we go through such an experience. We can be honest with Father about how we are feeling and what we are going through, recognising that it is something that we are "going through" – not a permanent condition. We can call for his help and trust his never ending loving purposes.

We can talk to Father in our own dialect. I can remember finding how precious that was to me. At a service in London, the musician leading the meeting said something like, "Take some time now to talk to Father in your own tongue." I think I know what he meant, but it struck me that "my tongue", the way of speaking that I grew up using was the north east Scotland local Portessie village version of what is sometimes called "Doric", and I rarely if ever used it in prayer. At school and in church we were expected to speak "proper English", and I remember just one man particularly who stuck to his "own tongue" when speaking in church. So at that service in London I began speaking to my Father , "mi Dad" in my childhood dialect and found how special that is.

9) EXPRESSION OF RELEASE

Luke 23v46

And when Jesus had cried out with a loud voice, he said, "Father, I place my spirit into your hands", and having said this he breathed out. Matthew uses the phrase meaning he "sent away" his spirit. John uses the phrase meaning he "gave over" his spirit. Mark and Luke use the phrase "breathed out" . The word *pneuma* can mean breath and can also mean spirit. The two are linked. As his last breath left him, so did his spirit.

This short sentence to Father comes after the time of darkness and the cry of "My God, my God why...?", Jesus spoke out, "It is finished" (John 19v30), and then makes this final statement. It is different from other prayers, as it is not a request for Father to do something, it is a statement to Father of what he, Jesus is doing. We can see the difference if we compare it with the similar situation in Acts 7v59 where Stephen requests in prayer, "Lord Jesus, receive my spirit."

Jesus' statement shows, and it is meant to show us, that whatever experience of isolation and suffering he had endured on the cross, he was still in close fellowship with Father. Instead of life being drained from him by the actions of others, he shows that just as he had given himself into that suffering, now that it was accomplished, he was still "in charge" of what was happening. When he states his decision to place his spirit into Father's hands, immediately with his last breath, his spirit leaves. His words show too that death was not the end. His body was dead indeed – but his spirit was in Father's hands.

Some people react to personal suffering by distancing themselves from relationship with God. We have a Father who never stops loving us, and is always within touching distance for us to put things into his hands.

There are situations, as Jesus showed at another time, that it is right to ask Father, and to keep on asking. There are also times when instead of asking, we can leave whatever we are concerned about in Father's care – to place it into His hands – and leave it there.

"Father, into your hands I place my spirit" is a good prayer for just before going to sleep.

CHURCH IS FAMILY
IN ACTS

INTRODUCTION

Let me take us now on an exploration through the book of Acts where we find the history of the early church to guide us as an example in living as a family. We might find that comparing it with what we are used to in church life will mean that we will have some rethinking to do.

We will see that the idea of "family" and God's people being brothers and sisters is not a new concept used only by the church, but is also used in the relationships of the Jewish community.

We will find that among all the interchangeable words used for followers of Jesus, "brothers" is the word used commonly for their relationship with one another, and that "church" and "brothers" are used to describe the same group of followers of Jesus.

(As has been shown earlier, the words in Greek for brother and sister are the same word with a different ending, so when "brothers" is used, it can refer to brothers and sisters.)

We will look at what church life was like and see that it was the life of people living in family relationship with one another.

Churches often have a differentiation of how "leaders" relate to others in the church, and how other "church members" relate to one another. People in the church are often defined by these relationships. We will look at how the apostles and other "leaders" related to the church family. This links to decision-making in the church family. Often in churches there are clear demarcations of who are the decision-makers on particular aspects of church life.

We will see the variety of ways that decisions were made in the church family in Acts.

1) THE JEWISH FAMILY

Before looking at the Church family in Acts, there is another "family" that is referred to by the apostles Peter and Paul - the "Jewish family".

In Acts 2v29 Peter, in addressing the crowd spoke to them as "men, brothers". Who was he addressing in this way? devout (v5), Judeans and all who live in Jerusalem (v 14), Israelites (v22). This was Peter's "family" – he is not an outsider to them; he is part of the same community.

The people respond in the same way to Peter and the apostles as "men, brothers" (v37).

Peter in Acts 3v17 addresses the "men of Israel" as "brothers" - the Old Testament family of God's people - and he mentions Moses' prophecy about Jesus as "one of your brothers" (v22).

In Acts 13v15 in Antioch of Pisidia, the ruler of the synagogue asked Paul and Barnabas to speak, addressing them as "men, brothers". When addressing these fellow-Jews, Paul addresses them too (13v26) as "men, brothers – children of the stock of Abraham", and again as "men, brothers" (13v38).

Paul addresses (in Hebrew dialect) his fellow Jews as "men, brothers and fathers" (Acts 22v1), the council as "men brothers" (23v1), and Jewish leaders as "men brothers" (28v17).

Peter and Paul make it clear that they are not departing from their Jewish family in joining the Church family. While Peter and Paul were identifying as "Jewish brothers", they were not saying that the Jewish family and Jesus' church family are the same thing.

Rather, they were encouraging their Jewish brothers to become Christian brothers.

They were showing that you did not have to leave the Jewish family to be in the Church family.

They were showing too that a person did not have to be in the Jewish family to be in the Church family.

So it is possible to be in the Jewish family and not be in the Jesus family.

It is also possible to be in the Jewish family and in the Jesus family.

It is also possible to be in the Jesus family without being in the Jewish family.

2) ONE FAMILY

The apostle Paul wants the readers of his letters to know that both people who are Jews and people from other nations can be in Father's family, together with one another.

In Romans 9v24-26 he writes (quoting the prophet Hosea in the Old Testament) that people who were at one time not considered to be included, are, together with those from the Jews, called "my people", "my loved one", and "sons of the living God".

In Galatians 3v26-27 he writes that his readers are, "all sons of God through faith in Christ Jesus", and that there is no distinction between Jew and Greek, slave and free, male and female, for "you are all one in Christ Jesus."

In Ephesians 2 Paul explains the breaking down of distinction between Jews and others by Jesus' death. He is our peace who has made both one, and has broken down the dividing wall between us... (v14) He came and preached peace to you who were far off and to those who were near... for through him we both have access by the one Spirit to the Father ... members of God's household (v17,18).

So Paul is showing us that while God has always had a special place and calling in His purposes for the Jewish nation, He has one family – made up of those from the Jewish nation and those from other nations who trust in who Jesus is and in what he has done to make it possible for us to be in Father's family.

3) THE CHRISTIAN FAMILY

Followers of Jesus are described in Acts using quite a range of terms. In just one chapter, Acts 9 we have the following: Saul threatening **disciples of the Lord** (v1) and looking for any **of this Way** (v2). Ananias is a certain **disciple** (v1) and he speaks to God about your **saints** in Jerusalem (v13) and when God sends him to Saul, he greets him as **brother** Saul (v17).

Saul spent some days with **the disciples** at Damascus (v19). When Jews in Damascus were seeking to kill Saul, **the disciples** helped him escape (v25). When Saul went to Jerusalem and tried to join the **disciples** they were afraid and did not believe he was a **disciple** (v26).

When Saul's life was threatened again, when they learned about it, **the brothers** arranged for him to go elsewhere (v30) Then **the church** had a time of peace throughout all Judea, Galilee and Samaria (v31). Peter went to **the saints** who lived at Lydda (v32). There was at Joppa a certain **disciple** – Tabitha/Dorcas who died (v36). The **disciples** at Joppa sent for Peter who brought her back to life (v38). Peter called **the saints** and the widows together to see Dorcas alive (v41) and as result many in the area **believed in the Lord** (v42).

In Acts 11v26 Barnabas and Saul met with the **church** and taught great numbers of people. The **disciples** were called **Christians** first at Antioch (v26) and the **disciples**....decided to provide help for the **brothers** in Judea (v29).

In Acts 18v18 Paul took leave of **the brothers** in Corinth, at Caesarea he greeted **the church** (v22) and he travelled – strengthening all **the disciples** (v23). When Apollos wanted to pass into Achaia, **the brothers** wrote, exhorting **the disciples** to receive him, and when he had come he helped **those who had believed through grace.** (v27)

So followers of / believers in Jesus were called:

- **disciples** – showing their relationship to Jesus

- **brothers** – showing their relationship to one another

- **church** – showing their togetherness in a place or in action

- **saints/ believers** – showing the distinction between them and those who were not disciples/brothers/ church

- **Christians** – by those outside who recognised that what made them identifiable was their relationship with Jesus, and dealt with them as such.

[The word for "called" in "called Christians" is an unusual word *chrematizo*. I like the way that Vine's expository Dictionary puts it : "Its primary significance is to have business dealings with.. They 'were (publicly) called' Christians because this was their chief business."!]

So we can see that "the disciples", "the brothers" and "the church" can be interchangeable terms – as is illustrated well in Acts 14v22,23 where Paul and Barnabas strengthened **the disciples**, appointing elders in every **church**, then they gathered **the church**, (v27) stayed a long time with **the disciples** and then certain men came and taught **the brothers** (15v1).

This definition of church as family is seen right from the beginning:

In Acts 1v13,14 we read that among those gathered in the first "church" of about 120 people were the apostles, the women who had followed him from Galilee (Luke23v49), and Jesus' mother and brothers. In the next verse, Acts 1v15 is the first reference to the whole company there of Jesus' people. Luke writes that Peter stood up in the middle of **"the brothers"**, so the first description of the church refers to their family relationship, and **brothers** is used of their relationship with one another throughout the New Testament.

4) FAMILY LIFE

Since "church is family", we can expect that relationship to be expressed in the life of the first church as it is described in Acts – and it is.

In Acts 2v1-4, they, that is the 120, were all together in one place, and the coming of the Holy Spirit in power was a "family experience" – it was something that they <u>all</u> experienced.

In Acts 2v17,18 Peter, quoting the prophecy of Joel, describes what is happening as an "all-age" family experience – including children (sons and daughters), youth and elderly, male and female.

From the 120 there was increase of 3000, and one might wonder how such a large group can be "managed" or organised. The relationship they came into was a family relationship as can be seen in the description of their life in Acts 2v42-46:

They were committed to *koinonia* – the fellowship – togetherness. They prayed together. They shared everything together. They cared for one another by selling possessions to provide for those in need. They spent time with each other daily in the temple courts and in having meals with one another in their homes. And this would have all come from the apostles' teaching which they were putting into practice together.

After the growth to more than 5000 in Acts 4v4, once again the description is that of family relationship. "They were one in heart and soul." They had things of their own, but they did not say that they were their own – they were part of the family possessions – they had everything "together". This is a reflection of normal family home life, where personal possessions are there for other family members to use and enjoy.

In Acts 4v34-36, again we see the willingness of people to sell houses or lands they owned in order to meet the needs of what must have been many poor people. This family care is further seen in Acts 6 with the appointing of seven people to make sure that all the widows and others in need were looked after every day. Acts 6v1 mentions that the distribution was daily.

The church was not just seen as a local family. In Acts 11v27,28 when a coming famine was predicted by a prophet, the Christians in Antioch decided to send from their prosperity financial help to who are described as "the brothers living in Judea" which was about 300 miles from Antioch.

They knew how to be a family!

5) CHURCH TODAY?

To see how far we might have strayed from our beginnings, imagine an unlikely scenario of a large group of completely new Christians today who have not had any previous personal background experience in church life. Without any knowledge of the church in Acts, they get together to decide how they should "do church" by looking just at the example of other existing churches. Here are the questions they might come up with:

Should we have a pope, a primate or a primus, archbishops, bishops, vicars and curates, priests, rector and vestry, minister and deacons, area superintendents, circuit stewards, elders, overseers, committees, leadership teams, councils, clergy and laity, apostles, prophets, evangelists, pastors and teachers or pastor-teachers?

What should we have in our services? Liturgy set by a book – which book?, Order of service set by one person, a group or an extemporary service? Who is allowed to participate? What music – what instruments – if any? Who chooses the hymns or songs or psalms – preacher, organist, musicians, members of congregation? Should there be a choir?

Where and when should we stand, sit, kneel? Should we move around? raise hands? clap? dance?

How long should a service last? When should it be held? How many should we have?

How is money going to be raised? How is it going to be spent? Who should decide?

How should we do Holy communion / Eucharist / Lord's supper / Breaking of Bread? What has to be done? Who can do what? What should be used? An uncut loaf, pre-diced bread, wafers, unleavened bread, alcoholic wine, non-alcoholic wine, choice of either, grape juice, blackcurrant squash (or other red drink). One cup, many cups? Who is allowed to administer it? Who is allowed to take it?

Where should we meet? Should we have a building of our own? If so what should it look like? How will it be paid for?

How much should we have to do with other churches who do things differently from us?

If this imaginary group of new Christians looked solely at the examples of what is considered important by different types of existing churches, I wonder how long it would be before they ever came to consider this as their fundamental question:

"How can we live as a family? God's family. Jesus' family."

2. LEADERSHIP RELATIONSHIP AND DECISION MAKING

1) PETER

After Jesus was taken up into heaven, in the first meeting of the church family in Acts 1v15, Peter stands up among the <u>brothers</u>, taking responsibility for giving a lead. Note that when Peter spoke he did not say, "As I am the specially appointed leader and apostle commanded by Jesus to shepherd the flock…", he simply said, "Men, brothers…" In speaking to them as brothers, he was putting himself in the relationship of brother to brother. He was speaking to the family of which he was a member.

Peter took a lead in applying God's Word to the situation relating to the issue of Judas and his replacement. He said what should be done, but he did not make the decision about who would be appointed. He said it should be someone who had been with them from the beginning, but then we read, so <u>they</u> (not Peter) proposed two men (v23) , and <u>they</u> prayed that God would make clear <u>His</u> choice, and they drew lots to discover who that was - Matthias, and he was then counted as one of the twelve apostles (v24-26).

2) GROWING CHURCH FAMILY

The next "church meeting", described at the influx of 3000 new believers on the day of Pentecost, shows the apostles as:

- Spokesmen for the church. "Peter standing up with the eleven lifted up his voice and said..."(2v14).

- Teachers of the church. "They continued steadfastly in the apostles' teaching" (2v42).

- Demonstrators of Jesus' kingdom power "Many miracles and signs were done by the apostles" (2v43).

The description of church life is of the ingredients of the life of a family – fellowship, meals together, praying together, being one in heart and soul and sharing their belongings. It does not say that the apostles organised all the activities, but that the church family expressed their new relationship with one another in the life they led.

This becomes clear in 4v32-35 where people who had lands or houses sold them to support those in need. That this was a completely voluntary personal choice is seen in Peter's statement to Ananias about the possession he sold but then lied about; "While you had it, was it not your own? And after it was sold was it not in your own authority?" (5v14). In other words, you were free to do what you chose with it, sell it or keep it, give the money or keep it.

3) APOSTLES' LEADERSHIP

While the giving was personal and freely given, at this point in the church family life, the proceeds were given to the apostles to decide on its distribution, so the apostles were in charge of the family's corporate finances. This changed after "more believers were added to the Lord, multitudes of men and women" (5v14). "And in those days when the number of disciples was multiplied" (6v1), there was discontent that some widows were being missed out in the daily giving out of resources to those in need. At this point, the apostles decide to hand over the family's finances to others in order to leave themselves the time and the freedom to fulfil their particular apostolic responsibilities which they describe as "prayer and the ministry of the word".

Like Peter did in Acts 1, the apostles together say to the church what should be done, but they don't do it themselves, they give the decision making to the family." Wherefore, <u>brothers, you</u> look out seven men - trustworthy, full of the Holy Spirit and wisdom, who <u>we</u> may appoint over this business" (6v3). So the multitude chose the seven (we are not told how they chose them). <u>They</u> set them before the apostles, and when they had prayed for them, they laid hands on them to pass on to them the responsibility for a major part of the church family's finances.

When the apostles who were in Jerusalem heard that Samaria had received the word of God, <u>they </u>sent Peter and John to them (Acts 8v14). So it was not just Peter and John deciding to go, but a decision of the apostles together that someone should go, and that it should be Peter and John.

4) FAMILY DECISIONS

In Acts 9, when Ananias (not the same one as in chapter 5!) is instructed by God to go and see Saul who had been an enemy of the church, he greets him as "brother Saul" He does not say, Believer Saul, or Convert Saul, or New Disciple Saul, or specially chosen Apostle Saul, but "Saul brother". It's a "Welcome to the family!"

Saul moved from Damascus to be with the apostles and was there until there was a plot to kill him, and we read that when <u>the brothers</u> knew, <u>they</u> brought him down to Caesarea (on the coast) and sent him away to Tarsus (9v30), so this was not just Saul going back "home", but a church family decision to send him there. We are not told why.

When news came to the church in Jerusalem that many people were becoming Christians in Antioch, <u>they </u>– that is the church in

Jerusalem - sent Barnabas to encourage what was happening there (Acts 11v22), and with even more growth, Barnabas decided to fetch Saul from Tarsus to assist at Antioch where they taught together for the next year (v25,26).

We are then introduced to a different aspect of decision making when a prophet, Agabus prophesies the coming of a great famine. On hearing this, "the disciples, everyone according to their ability decided to send relief to the brothers who lived in Judea (v29).

- So, the decision to give was a family one - "the disciples"

- how much to give was an individual decision - "Everyone according to their ability"

- and the decision to send Barnabas and Saul with the gift was a family one - "they sent it", and they sent it to "the elders" in the church family at Jerusalem. (This is the first introduction we have to some in the church family being described as elders.)

5) GOD'S DECISIONS

We have reminders in various places that the decision making was not just that of the human members of the church family: in choosing the replacement apostle, they asked for God's decision. The money sent from Antioch was as a result of a prophetic revelation, and in Acts 13v2, while the prophets and teachers in the Antioch church were serving the Lord and fasting, the Holy Spirit made known to them that His decision was for them to set apart Barnabas and Saul for the work He had called them to do, so they fasted and prayed and released them to do that. They went on a journey, preaching, planting churches and appointing elders for every church (14v23).

6) APOSTLES, ELDERS AND FAMILY DECISION

In Acts 15 we have a fascinating and informative account about the relationships of church leaders with the church, church leaders to other church leaders, and the church family to other parts of the church family.

It began with men coming to the church at Antioch from Judea teaching "the brothers" that they could not be saved without being circumcised. The Jerusalem church family made it clear that they had not been sent by them (v24). Paul and Barnabas disagreed with this circumcision teaching, and the argument that followed did not lead to agreement in the church family. So they that is "the brothers" decided to send Paul and Barnabas, and some others of the Antioch church family to Jerusalem to the apostles and elders there.

It is interesting that they sent others with Paul and Barnabas. Perhaps this would give confidence to the church that the report from Jerusalem would not be just the well-known views of Paul and Barnabas on the subject. It would also convey to those in Jerusalem the perspective of those who were part of the church family at Antioch.

It says that they were "helped on their way by the church" whom they shared with in different places on their journey, telling them about the conversion of the Gentiles and causing great joy to all "the brothers" (v3). (not involving them in the matter of dispute they were going to Jerusalem to resolve!)

They were received by the church family, the apostles and the elders. We know who the apostles were, but we are not told here who in the church family were recognised as "elders".

The apostles and elders came together to consider the issue. It was a doctrinal issue (the main responsibility of the apostles), and also a pastoral issue (the main responsibility of the elders).

After a lot of argument, apostle Peter gets up to speak, and it looks like the discussion of apostles and elders was happening in the hearing of the whole church family, as it says that following Peter rising up and saying to "them" – the apostles and elders, then all the multitude kept silence and listened to Barnabas and Saul (v12). Peter as before, addresses his hearers as "men/

brothers", shares his testimony of seeing Gentiles receiving the Holy Spirit and gives the definitive doctrinal statement, "We believe that through the grace of the Lord Jesus Christ we shall be saved, even as they are" (v11).

Barnabas and Saul having given their accounts to the church family of their ministry among the Gentiles, are followed by elder James who, as Peter did, speaks as brother to brothers, and gives a pastoral answer to what should be done about the issue.

Who is this James? It is important to know who he is, and what his relationship is to leadership and the Family.

He is not the apostle James, brother of John, as he had been put to death by Herod (Acts 12v2).

There is an indication that he was a leader in the church family in Acts 12v17 when Peter, after his angel-led escape from prison tells the prayer meeting in the house he went to, to tell "James and the brothers."

Along with the leadership role James exercises in chapter 15, this is further confirmed later in Acts 21v18 when Luke, the writer of Acts and companion of Paul, says that they came to Jerusalem, were received gladly by "the brothers" and the next day they went to see James, and all the elders were present.

We learn the identity of this James from what Paul writes in Galatians. He says in Galatians 1v19, that following his own conversion he was not in any contact with the apostles until three years later when he went to Jerusalem where he saw Peter, but did not see any of the other apostles – only James – the Lord's brother. (mentioned in Matthew 13v55). We can see that James was in the church family from the beginning as in Acts 1, among those who were gathered together were "Mary the mother of Jesus, and with his brothers" (1v14).

Then there is the interesting description Paul gives in Galatians 2v9 when he is again in Jerusalem and in telling the church of his ministry to the Gentiles, he says "And when James, Peter and John who seemed to be pillars perceived the grace that was given to me, they gave me the right hand of fellowship..."

This is a unique description of church leaders. He does not say "Those who were in control" or "those who told me that they were the leaders – the decision-makers", but simply "those who seemed to be pillars". In other words, they were not self-promoting, but by their words and actions gave the impression that they were depended on for the structure and stability of the church family.

And then, this same James is the one who wrote the letter on practical Christian living which bears his name, and his description of himself as "a servant / slave of God and of the Lord Jesus Christ." (James 1v1)

So, now back to Acts 15, where James as leading elder gives the lead in saying, "I judge...." (v19) and this finds agreement with the apostles, and elders, and the whole church family and there is a joint decision send representatives of their family with Barnabas and Paul to Antioch. They send Judas Barsabbas and Silas – who are described as "leading men in/among the brothers." Something of what that means is seen the description of them along with Barnabas and Paul in the letter to Antioch as "men who have given over their lives for the name of our Lord Jesus Christ" (v26), and prophets who were able to strengthen others through their encouragement (v32).

It is interesting to see that these two, having been "sent off / released" by the Jerusalem church to go to Antioch (v30), once they had strengthened the church, the church decided to "send off/release" them to be free to go back to the apostles (v33). That shows that they were understood to be there on a mission on behalf of the apostles, and also that they were there serving the church at Antioch until the church family decided to release them from that responsibility. Silas freely made the personal choice to stay with them (v34).

It is worth noting too that the letter is sent headed: (from) The apostles and the elders, brothers (to) the Gentile brothers. So it is written accepting the Gentile believers as being in the family, and having the same status as themselves as brothers and sisters.

7) AN APOSTLE'S INITIATIVE AND FAMILY RESTRAINT

In Acts 19, we see apostle Paul independently taking the initiative in what he intends to do: Paul decided to go to Jerusalem, passing through Macedonia and Achaia. "After I have been there," he said, "I must visit Rome also"(v21). But later in the chapter we find that when he wants to confront opposition in Ephesus: "the disciples there would not let him", and other influential friends persuaded him against it (v30). So even the apostle was not independent of church family decisions.

8) ROLES AND RESPONSIBILITIES OF THOSE IN LEADERSHIP IN THE CHURCH

We can see in the experience of the church in Acts that there is an emphasis on <u>family decisions</u>, helped by the apostles in their responsibility - prayer and the ministry of the Word (Acts 6v4), and elders in theirs - shepherds of God's flock in their care (1 Peter 5v2).

The leaders, in their communications with the church, always speak as brothers to brothers expressing their family relationships.

It is striking that the only times when the apostles are instructing the church to do something, they are telling <u>them </u>– the family to make the decision (Acts 1v21-26, Acts 6v3), and instead of keeping leadership decisions to themselves, they are happy to hand over the responsibility of the financial pastoral care of the family to others (Acts 6v3).

ELDERS

The word elder means simply "those who are older", and is used then and now by different groups and cultures with widely varying application of what that term implies. It is important for us to see not what the term meant for the Jews or other nations, or how the term is used by different denominations or churches today, but to see what responsibility that description meant in the churches of Acts. Fortunately we have in Acts 20v28-32 a clear description of elders' responsibilities when Paul is speaking to the elders of the church in Ephesus.

He begins by saying what literally means "have near" – this is translated as "take heed" or "watch over". I think that a better phrase which would fit all the times where these words are used would be "pay close attention to". This close attention is not just to be given to the "others" in the church, but also to themselves, to each other as elders, recognising as he indicates, that they too may potentially go astray (v30).

They are to pay close attention to all the flock, to take an interest in the welfare of each one, not leaving any one out.

In the next phrase we enter the area of how translators use words to accord with their view of church. In the King James AV, the next phrase reads "the flock over which the Holy Ghost hath made you overseers" implying a superiority of the elders' position above others in the church. But the word which is rendered "over" here is the Greek word *en* which means simply in or among, and as The Companion Bible note on this verse emphatically points out, ["Out of 2622 occurrences of *en*, it is rendered "over" only here!"] So elders are to pay close attention to the flock in which the Holy Spirit has given them a particular responsibility of care. We might say, they may be shepherds, but they are also sheep.

So we note here, that correctly understood and applied, elders are those who have a calling and equipping from the Holy Spirit which is necessary for fulfilling their responsibility. The word used for their appointment is that they have been "placed " by the Holy Spirit. God has placed every one of them in the body as it has pleased Him (1 Corinthians 12v18).

Now what are they placed as? The word used does mean to look or to watch over, so the common English translation as overseer is accurate but can be misleading as that word is used in English in a way that is different from the meaning here.

The Concise Oxford English dictionary defines oversee as: supervise (a person or their work) and supervise as : observe and direct the execution (of a task or activity) or the work of (a person). That does not accurately define the responsibility of elders.

The Revised Standard Version's use of "guardians" and the Good News Bible's use of "the flock the Holy Spirit has placed in your care" accord with what being an overseer is described as in the next phrase, "To shepherd/feed the church of God."

Some translations put "Be shepherds of" but there is no noun, it is a verb – the emphasis is not on who they are but on what they are to do for others. What are the responsibilities of shepherding? To feed the flock, bringing them to good pasture, to take care of their welfare, and to protect them from harm. And so in being warned about "wolves" which will seek to attack their flock, the elders are advised to "Watch" – the word means to be awake – so to see potential threats and to protect the church from them.

APPOINTING ELDERS

In Acts 14v23, we read of Paul and Barnabas appointing elders in the churches they were visiting. The word used is the word *cheirotoneo* which Vine's Expository Dictionary of New Testament Words says was "primarily used of voting in the Athenian legislative assembly and meaning to stretch forth the hands".

From Acts 20v28, we saw that it is the Holy Spirit who places people as elders, so here as Vine's continues "had appointed i.e. by the recognition of those who had been manifesting themselves as gifted of God to discharge the functions of elders." So they were affirming them publicly for that responsibility.

APOSTLES, ELDERS, THE SEVEN (Acts 6)

There is a common tendency to view different leadership roles as separate from each other and in a particular order of seniority, but this is not borne out by what is said of them in Acts.

Firstly – the Seven. There is nothing about them in the passage or anywhere else in the New Testament which makes any connection of their position with that of those recognised elsewhere as "servants/servers"(1Timothy 3v8) sometimes translated "deacons" with all the associations that has in present day churches.

There is nothing to say that these men were not already elders as they clearly had spiritual maturity, and when in Acts 11v30 money was being sent from Antioch to Jerusalem to "the elders", administering the distribution of that gift was the kind of responsibility that the seven had.

More than that, in the life of the church in Acts, the distinctive comment made about the apostles was that many wonders and signs were done by the apostles"(2v43). It is of significance that immediately after the choosing of the seven, that two of them are mentioned and their ministries are described. They are not restricted to practical administration. Rather, Stephen is described as "full of faith and power, did great wonders and signs among the people" (6v8) – and then gives in his preaching a clear explanatory summary of the Old Testament. Then Philip, when he went preaching in a new area like the apostles did, the people of Samaria took notice of what he said "hearing and seeing the signs which he did" (8v6).

So while these two were not of the twelve, they had similar attributes to them. There is no title or name given to the seven as a group; instead we are told of a job they were to do for the family. Apostolic eldership might be a suitable description of their ministry.

SERVANT LEADERSHIP

It might be thought that apostles are in some way senior to elders because apostles Barnabas and Paul appointed elders in the churches. But then we have to remember that it was the church family who first chose who could be one of the original apostles (Acts 1v23), so these appointments are not indicative of seniority but of recognition of God-given responsibilities.

In Acts 15 when apostles and elders are mentioned, it is clear that there were elders as distinct from the 12 apostles (or rather 11 after apostle James' death Acts 12v2). This is clear because James (the brother of Jesus) is mentioned and he was not one of the apostles, so we can count him as an elder. And the letter goes out from the apostles and the elders. However, they are not completely separate groups, as Peter in 1 Peter 5, giving similar instructions to elders as Paul did in Acts 20, describes himself as an elder (v1), and we see that one of his particular apostolic responsibilities given to him by Jesus was to shepherd the flock (John 21v15,16). So going back to the first mention of elders in the Jerusalem church family in Acts 11v30, the term there, as well as perhaps including some of the seven would probably include the apostles.

And to dispel any thoughts that servants/ helpers in the church are something less than elders or apostles, Peter in Acts 1 describes the sphere of the twelve apostles as that of serving. Judas "was numbered with us and had obtained part of this serving" (v17), and the church prayed for the one who would "take part of this serving and apostleship"(v25). As we will see in the letters that the apostles wrote, they describe themselves as servants. "Paul, a servant of Jesus Christ and an apostle" (Romans 1v1). "Simon Peter, a servant and apostle of Jesus Christ (2 Peter 1v1).

The church we see in Acts is not an institution governed by a system of rules for decision making, not a religious organisation led by people with hierarchical titles or special clothes to signify their status or authority over others, but rather an ever growing missionary family of people taking on their God-given responsibilities to take care of one another and to extend the family by introducing others to Father and His Son. In fact they appeared to simply follow Jesus' instructions about how they should behave in not being like the rulers of the heathen having power over people, and leaders having complete authority. Rather, to be great, they must be the servant of the rest, and if one wants to be first, he must be their slave – like the Son of Man, who did not come to be served, but to serve and to give his life to redeem many people (Matthew 20v25).

3. NAMES AND MEANINGS

Seeing the roles and responsibilities of those in leadership in the church family in Acts – the apostles, elders and the seven in chapter 6 - raises the question of how terms that are commonly used in some churches today relate to this.

1) PRIEST – There is nowhere in the New Testament the designation of "priest" to any individual in the church. There are three places where "priests" is a designation given as a collective name to everyone in the church. Revelation 1v6 speaks of Jesus making us kingdom priests to God, and Revelation 5v9,10 describes kingdom priests from every tribe, language, people and nation to reign on the earth. Revelation 20v6 says of those who have part in the first resurrection that they will be priests of God and Christ and shall reign with him a thousand years.

There are also two places where the term priesthood is used. 1 Peter 2v5 describes us as stones being built into a spiritual house, a holy priesthood to offer spiritual sacrifices acceptable to God by Jesus Christ. 1 Peter 2v9 speaks of a chosen generation, a kingdom priesthood, a holy nation, God's people to proclaim, to broadcast the truth about God.

Jesus' role as High Priest and how that relates to the Jewish priesthood is explained in the letter to Hebrews.

2) BISHOP – The title "bishop" is used by a number of denominations to designate someone with a particular leadership role, status and relationship to others in the church.

In some New Testament translations such as King James AV, the word bishop is used in some places to translate the word *episkopos* which means literally an overseer – someone who watches over.

In Philippians 1v1 Paul and Timothy write to all the saints in Christ Jesus at Philippi along with bishops/overseers and deacons/servants. We see here that the word was used not of one individual in the church but of number of people.

1 Timothy 3v1 says that if anyone desires bishopping/overseeing (there is no "the office of" in the Greek) he desires a good <u>work</u>. So it refers to a job to be done rather than a position or status, and the job requirements are then given. A bishop/overseer must be…

In Titus 1v5-7 Paul instructs Titus to appoint <u>elders </u>in every city, then begins a description of them and continues, "for a bishop/overseer must be…" clearly indicating that elders and bishops/overseers are the same people.

In 1 Peter 5v2 Peter instructs the <u>elders</u> to shepherd the flock "taking the *episkope* oversight of them."

In Acts 20v28 Paul speaks to <u>elders </u>of the flock in which the Holy Spirit "has made you overseers." (the same word as translated elsewhere "bishops").

So in the New Testament, this word "overseer" is the work description of elders.

The Jerusalem Bible (produced by the Roman Catholic Church which of course has bishops) accurately points out in a note about 1Timothy 3v1 "The word *episkopos* used here by Paul, had not yet acquired the same meaning as "bishop").

3) DEACON AND MINISTER

Although these words are different designations from one another and are used to mean different things in different denominations, we need to look at them together as they are both translations of the same work in Greek *diakonos* which means "servant".

The word *diakonos* is used in a variety of ways, for example:

- the ordinary use in John 2 of the servants filling the jars with water at the wedding at Cana.

- Paul's description of himself and others as God's servants. (1 Corinthians 3v5, Colossians 1v7, 4v7, 1 Thessalonians 3v2)

- and as servants of the New Covenant (2 Corinthians 3v6),

- servants of the Gospel (Ephesians 3v6,7; Colossians 1v23).

- Then in the translations where the word "deacon" is used, it appears in Philippians 1v1 writing to the saints in Christ Jesus along with "bishops and deacons" – or "overseers and servants."

We know that overseers signifies elders, and we can take it from this greeting (which only occurs here) that there was also a group of people who were working for the church. We are given no clue here concerning what responsibilities they had, other than that they were recognised in their responsibility for some aspect of the church's work.

The presence of such a group of people is indicated in 1 Timothy 3v8-13, where again, while the word deacon is used in translations, the word is *diakonos* – servant. The quality of the life and Christian commitment of these church workers is to be similar to those accepted as elders. Once again there is no definition of any particular area of serving that is described, unlike the various definitions of "deacon" that different churches use to describe that role, and 1Timothy 3v13 seems to suggest that the outcome of their work is them gaining a standing for the flow of the Gospel.

We do have one description of someone who appears to have served in such a role, and the particular type of service she was engaged in.

In Romans 16v1 Paul, in writing to the church at Rome commends to them "Phoebe, our sister, who is a servant of the church at Cenchrea." Cenchrea was near Corinth, so it looks like Phoebe has travelled with this letter. The believers at Rome are urged to receive her and help her in any way she needs as she has been a *prostatis* of many and of Paul too. *Prostatis* means literally someone who stands in front or before. It means a leader, a protector – someone who has stood up for others. While we do not know the details of what that meant in her significant service for the church, we can get some hint from the use of that role outside the New Testament. [*Prostates* was the title of a citizen of Athens who had the responsibility of seeing to the welfare of resident aliens who were without civic rights. Among the Jews it signified a wealthy patron of the community. (Vine's Expository dictionary of New Testament words).]

So whatever the kind of work responsibility that church deacons/servants were engaged in, they were not restricted to helping in church services, or looking after buildings and finance.

4) MINISTER

Some churches use the word minister in particular ways which are not seen in the New Testament, except to say that if, when it is used, it is recognising that person as a servant of God and the Gospel, then it is entirely in keeping with its Biblical use.

So churches who have minister and deacons, have a servant and servants!

5) PASTOR

The designation, "Pastor" has particular meanings and job descriptions when it is used by churches. This can mask the way that the word is used in the New Testament.

The word *poimen* appears 18 times in the New Testament. It is translated "shepherd" 17 times, and only once as "pastor" – and it is interesting that in 9 English Bible translations that I have, in all but one they use the word pastor in Ephesians 4v11 – apostles, prophets, evangelists, pastors, and teachers. That is the only place "pastor" appears, and is the only place where *poimen* shepherd is describing someone in that role in the church. Only the Moffat translation puts it "some to shepherd".

This use of a different word from shepherd somehow seems to make a false distinction of what a "pastor" is, making it a title similar to using bishop when the word means overseer.

The verb *poimaino* to shepherd appears only three times in relation to the care of the church.

- Peter is instructed to <u>shepherd</u> Jesus' sheep (John 21v16).

- <u>Elders</u> are instructed to <u>shepherd</u> the church of God as they are <u>overseers</u> (Acts 20v28).

- <u>Elders</u> are instructed to <u>shepherd</u> the flock of God, taking <u>oversight</u> of it. (1 Peter 5v1)

Thus when it says in Ephesians 4v14 that some are shepherds it is referring to the work of elders in watching over the life and needs of the church family.

CHURCH IS FAMILY IN
THE LETTERS

The letters in the New Testament are viewed as authoritative texts on Christian doctrine, written by people who were especially inspired by the Holy Spirit for that task – and that of course is true. We can sometimes, therefore, perceive the writers as standing apart from, or even above their readers and us present day ordinary Christians – but that is not how they saw themselves. The letters they wrote are family correspondence, and one of the authoritative doctrines that appear over and over again throughout the letters is that "Church is family".

This can be seen in

1) How they describe themselves and other Christians, and how they address the people they are writing to.

2) What they say about relationship with Father and Jesus.

3) The church family instructions they give in the letters.

1. BROTHERS TO BROTHERS

Paul, while he introduces himself in 10 of his 12 letters in terms of the particular calling and responsibility he has been given as "apostle", he does not write in any of his letters as a leader of an organisation, but as a brother to brothers. In his letters he addresses his readers as "brothers" 64 times, and when speaking of other followers of Jesus he describes them as "brothers" 40 times, and he wrote of those who were with him sending these letters as brothers – Sosthenes (1 Corinthians), Timothy (2 Corinthians, Philippians, Colossians, 1 Thessalonians, 2 Thessalonians), and Silas/Silvanus (1 Thessalonians and 2 Thessalonians).

The unnamed writer to the Hebrews addresses his readers as brothers 4 times and describes others as brothers 4 times.

The term "brothers" is clearly special to the writer James as he addresses his readers in this way 15 times in the 5 chapters of his letter, and most often as "my brothers".

Peter too addressed his readers as "brothers" and mentions "our beloved brother, Paul" (2 Peter 3v15)

John writes of brothers too, but as an older man he writes to the family as "children" linking their relationship with him as "my dear children" to them being called "God's children" (1 John 3v1). Even though John is a senior apostle and received an astonishing revelation experience of and from Jesus, he addresses himself to the seven churches he is writing to simply as "I John, your brother" (Revelation 1v9).

It appears that throughout this family correspondence, there is a desire to emphasise that in the family of Jesus, no one is less than a brother or sister, and no one is more than a brother or sister.

2. FATHER AND JESUS

We will look here at how the writers write about The Father, Jesus' father, Our Father, Family likeness, Father.

1) THE FATHER

There are a few places in the letters, when speaking of "The Father" it is referring to something different from His relationship to Jesus or to us.

The Father of Creation.

In 1 Corinthians 8, Paul is writing about how idols may be called gods, but in reality there is only one God, and in saying who this God is, he says He is "the Father from whom all things came"(v6)– the Father of creation – father in the meaning that He is the originator of everything.

The Father of the whole concept of "family".

Where does the idea, the relationships and structure of "family" come from?

Ephesians 3v14 says "The Father from whom every family in heaven and earth derives its name." We know what "family" is from the reality of God being Father. We learn what it means to be a father and what it means to be a family from "The Father" and His relationship to his children.

The definition of family in the words used here indicate those who have the same father. The word for father in Greek is *pater* and the word translated family is *patria*. The other places this word is used in the New Testament is in Luke 2v4 where Joseph went to Bethlehem because he was "of the house and *patria* of David" – the family descended from David. In Acts 3v25 God's promise to Abraham is – " through your seed shall all the *patria* of the earth be blessed". From Abraham's family, all the other families would be blessed.

If we apply this to "Church is Family" it means Church is those fathered by God.

2) JESUS' FATHER

The relationship of Father and his Son, Jesus is seen throughout the letters.

Romans 1v1,2 begins by introducing God's Good News as concerning his Son, Jesus Christ, our Lord – a descendent of David but marked out as Son of God with power by being raised from death.

This is a recurring theme:

- His Son. (Romans 8v3, 1 Corinthians 1v9, 1 John 1v7)

- God has sent forth the Spirit of His Son. (Galatians 4v6)

- The kingdom of his loved Son. (Colossians 1v 12,13)

- From Father, glory and honour.. "This is my Son.." (2 Peter 1v17)

- The Son of God. (1 John 3v8)

- The Father sent the Son. (1 John 4v14)

- Both the Father and the Son. (2 John v9)

- The Father with his Son, Jesus Christ. (1 John 1v3)

- Father of our Lord Jesus Christ. (2 Corinthians 1v3, Ephesians 1v3, Colossians 1v3, 1 Peter 1v3)

- His Father. (Revelation 1v6)

The writer to the Hebrews writes to show the special, distinct and unique place that Jesus has as Son of the Father. As Son, he is distinct and different from the prophets (Hebrews 1v1-3). As Son he is distinct and different from the angels (1v5). As Son he is distinct and different from Moses (3v5,6). As Son he is distinct and different from those who had been high priest (4v14; 9v25,26).

John in his letter outlines the purpose of the Father sending his Son:– to destroy the works of the Devil (1 John 3v8) - and to be the Saviour of the world (1 John 4v14) . He also emphasises the crucial importance of recognising Jesus in his unique relationship as God's Son: Anyone who denies the special Father/Son relationship is an enemy of Jesus, and anyone who rejects Jesus having that relationship is rejecting his Father also (1 John 2v22).

Confirmation of the special Father/Son relationship is given by the words attributed to Father concerning Jesus:

"You are my Son". "I will be to him Father and He will be to me Son" (Hebrews 1v5), and the first-hand account of Peter recalling the experience on the mountain with Jesus, "For he received from Father God honour and glory when there came a voice… "This is my loved Son in whom I am well pleased" (2 Peter 1v17).

We are also given words attributed to Jesus about Father:

- "I will declare your name to my brothers " (Hebrews 2v12).

- " I will acknowledge him before my Father and his angels"(Revelation 3v5), restating what he had said before in Matthew 10v32 and Luke 12v8.

- "I have been victorious and now sit by my Father on His throne" (Revelation 3v21) – a position he had referred to in Matthew 19v28, Matthew 25v31, and when he had been asked if he was God's Son (Matthew 26v64).

This relationship of Father and Son is the heart and spring of all that the letter writers are saying, and of the family life, relationships, blessings and mission that flow from it.

3) OUR FATHER

We look now at where "Father" in the letters is described as "Our Father".

It is striking that Paul, in every letter he writes, begins with a reference to "our Father" and in what he says he makes clear his understanding of what flows to us from that relationship. He knows Father as a source of blessing to His children and he wants his readers to know, experience and receive all that Father has for them.

In his letters to each of the churches, Paul writes, "Grace to you, and peace from God our Father and the Lord Jesus Christ", (and in his letters to individuals – Timothy and Titus, he says the same and adds "mercy").

Along with this statement of what our Father is like – he is a grace and peace father – Paul expands each time on what this means in receiving from Him the blessings that our Father has for his children. Being blessed by our Father means:

- Being blessed with every spiritual blessing in heavenly places in Christ (Ephesians 1v3), and this includes:

- being loved and called (Romans 1v7)

- being enriched in word and knowledge (1 Corinthians 1v3)

- having Him alongside to help us (2 Corinthians 1v4)

- benefitting from all that Jesus did for us (Galatians 1v4)

- having our Father's commitment to complete what he has begun in us (Philippians 1v6)

- having a secured hope kept for us in heaven (Colossians 1v5)

- being chosen and receiving joy in the Holy Spirit (1 Thessalonians 1v4,6)

- having a promised ultimate freedom and peace from every trouble (2 Thessalonians 1v7)

4) KNOWING FATHER AS OUR FATHER

John in his first letter wants us to realise how wonderful it is that we can be Father's children. He writes " See what manner of – what kind of love the Father has given us" (1 John 3v1). The word used does not mean "how great" as in some translations, but what kind of – the primary meaning of the word is "from what country". The love that has been given to us in Jesus is the quality not of an earthly human love – but a love "from another country" – from heaven – and the purpose of that love being given is to bring us into Father's family so that we can rightly be called "God's children".

Paul, in Ephesians 1v4-7, shows us that placing us as His children in our relation to Jesus who has made it possible, has always been Father's plan.

In Romans 8 it is explained that it is by being given the Holy Spirit that we come into that special relationship as Father's children. That Spirit gives us our place. It then speaks of us addressing

Father as "Abba" – the Aramaic word used by a child. Galatians 4v4-7 has the same theme, saying that it is Jesus who has done what is needed for us to be placed as sons in receiving the Holy Spirit and crying "Abba – Father".

These are the only places in the New Testament that "Abba" is used apart from in Mark 14 v36 where Jesus uses it in his prayer in Gethsemane. In considering these verses it is important to note: Some translations have a "Spirit of adoption" and Galatians 4v5 "receiving the adoption of sons". This can be confusing as our use of the word "adopted" means one who did not come into the family by birth , but who was brought into it and accepted as a son or daughter.

The word used in the New Testament means "placed as a son" so when the word is used in these passages it means the placing of sons with the privileges and responsibilities and recognition that is implied. It is not about coming into the family, but rather our place in the family.

It is of note too that both passages speak of crying out, "Abba, Father". It signifies a loud expression.

So it is saying something more than when we are in Father's family we can call him, "Abba" – or whatever our family, cultural, language dialect equivalent is.

It may help our understanding to imagine these two scenes:

Firstly, imagine a family where the process of adopting a child has just been completed. The papers have been signed, the child has been received into the family's home. Because she is old enough to understand, the process and meaning of adoption is explained to her by the father who then says, "So you can now call me, 'Daddy'".

That is not what is being conveyed in the verses here. It is not a description of a formal permission being given because of the change of status of a person to be allowed to use this word (however special that may be!).

Now imagine a brother and sister, say 5 and 3 years old playing together on their own in their garden, then coming round the corner unexpectedly is their father. What do they do when they see him? They cry out, "Daddy!" (or Dada, or Papa or whatever equivalent family language/dialect word they use) and run towards him, arms open wide to hug and be hugged by him. It is an emotional exclamation of delighted recognition and gladness at his presence. As The Father's children we share in and express childlike delight in having Father as our Father.

God's activity has made a change in our lives – Romans 8 speaks of Him giving us the Holy Spirit. James 1v18 says that it is of God's own will he begat us – He chose to father us – to bring us to birth – with the word of truth so that we should be a kind of firstfruits of his creatures. 1 Peter 1v23 speaks of us having been born (or begotten) again not of corruptible seed, but of incorruptible by the living and abiding word of God. 1 John 3v9 speaks of God's seed abiding in those who are begotten from God.

These verses emphasise that we are not just accepted into God's family – we are born into that family by the activity of God in our lives, so that we are changed for ever. As Paul put it in 2 Corinthians 5v17, "Anyone who is in Christ is a new creation."

5) FAMILY LIKENESS

Since we are Father's children it is to be expected that we share and demonstrate a family likeness. That family likeness is characterised by purity and love.

Purity 2 Corinthians 6v17 speaks of us being a family that is different from those who are associated with wickedness, darkness, unbelief and idol worship. We are to be free from uncleanness as we are sons and daughters of Father, and we are to "purify ourselves from everything that contaminates body and spirit".

Love In Ephesians 4v32 we are encouraged to be kind and compassionate to one another, forgiving each other just as in Christ God has forgiven us – and so to "be imitators of God as dearly loved children and live a life of love, just as Christ loved us.." (5v1)

Love and Purity In 1 Thessalonians 3v12,13 Paul prays that the Lord will "make your love increase and overflow" and that he would "strengthen your hearts so that you will be blameless and holy in the presence of God our Father".

James 1v27 says that Father-likeness is seen in **Love**– giving focussed support to fatherless and widows, and **Purity** – keeping ourselves from being polluted by the world.

Purity 1 Peter 1v15-17 says that as obedient children we should be holy because Father is holy and **Love** we should love one another deeply (v22).

Purity and **Love** 1 John2v15 speaks of love for worldly things having no place in those who love the Father.

That **Purity** and **Love** which is in the Father's likeness is what He is committed to see grow, develop and be expressed in His children, and Hebrews 12v5-7 shows that Father is active in disciplining his children v10 "that we may share in his holiness" and it makes clear that this discipline expresses Father's love and acceptance of us.

There is another family likeness for us to take note of found in 1 John 4v4 which says, "You, dear children are from God and have overcome them, because "the One who is in you is greater than the one who is in the world". There is a confidence and a power that is available to us – in us because we are His family.

6) FATHER GOD

In looking at every place in the New Testament where Father is mentioned referring to God, I discovered something significant.

In speaking about God as father, the common term used is "the Father" which is usually a correct translation of the Greek, but I found a number of places where there was no "the" in the Greek, but there was still one in the English translations.

The occurrences are in the letters where Father is not being described or taught about, but where he is being named by those in the church family to others in the family. Here are the instances where, instead of "God the Father", it simply names "God Father", or to make more sense to us in English, he is being named as "Father God", so I have put the words in that order.

Here is what the verses say:

- Peace to the brothers and love with faith from Father God and Lord Jesus Christ. *(no the in either)* (Ephesians 6v23) - Not their descriptions but their names.

- that every tongue should confess that Lord Jesus Christ to glory of Father God (Philippians 2v11.

- to Timothy, my true child in the faith, grace, mercy, peace from Father God and Christ Jesus the Lord of us (1 Timothy 1v2).

- to Timothy my beloved child, grace, mercy, peace from Father God and Christ Jesus the Lord of us (2 Timothy 1v2).

- grace, mercy and peace from Father God and Christ Jesus the Saviour of us (Titus 1v4).

- strangers... elect according to the foreknowledge of Father God (1 Peter 1v2).

- For he received from Father God honour and glory when there came a voice.... "The son of me, the loved of me this is, in whom I am well pleased!" (2 Peter 1v17).

- John in 1 John and 2 John in his teaching about Father, 15 times refers to "the" Father, but in his family greeting he says: Grace, mercy peace from Father God and from Jesus Christ the son of the Father (2 John v3).

- to them that are loved by Father God (Jude v1).

The writers knew God not just as "the Father" as a title or description, but as "Father"- his name in relationship to them as children in His family.

3. CHURCH FAMILY INSTRUCTIONS

The New Testament letters are full of instructions for followers of Jesus on living as Christians, but here we will confine our investigation to instructions that are specifically about the Church family life and relationships as brothers and sisters.

These instructions seem to fit into these categories:

1) LOVE 2) CONSIDERATION 3) RESPONSIBILITY 4) PROVISION 5) DISCIPLINE AND CORRECTION 6) INTEGRITY 7) FAMILY GATHERINGS

1) LOVE

AN HONOURING LOVE: Romans 12v10 instructs us to have (*philostorgos*) family affection and brotherly love, being out front in honouring one another.

AN EXPANDING LOVE: In 1 Thessalonians 4v9 the readers don't need to be instructed in brotherly love as they have already learned that from God and are demonstrating it, not just in the local church family but in the wider region. The instruction to them and to us is to keep increasing in that love.

A PERMANENT LOVE: Hebrews 13v1 instructs us simply to let brotherly love continue/stay/abide. Brotherly love is meant to be a permanent characteristic of church family life.

AN EXTENDED LOVE: 1 Peter1v22 says that if our brotherly love is genuine then we should not be passive, but have love from our heart which is outstretched to our brothers and sisters.

AN INCLUSIVE LOVE: 1 Peter 2v17, among other instructions on Christian life, includes that we should love "the brotherhood" (*adelphotes*) – that means loving the whole family, not just particular or local members of it.

A SENSITIVE LOVE: 1 Peter 3v8 puts the instruction to be brotherly loving in a list of being in agreement, being sympathetic, tender-hearted and kindly-minded.

A SACRIFICIAL LOVE: 1 John 3v16 says that knowing the love that Jesus had in laying down his life for us should lead us to lay down our lives for our brothers and sisters. The word that is translated as something we "ought" to do, means that we owe it. When Jesus laid down his life, it meant for him, the cross. For us it may mean doing something for someone in the family that they would find it difficult to do, or carrying a burden to lighten the load for them, or giving our time to help them though a painful time. Whatever its application, it means putting the needs of brothers and sisters above our own, whatever the cost to us.

2) CONSIDERATION

CONSIDERATION OF DIFFERENCES

There are many wide-ranging differences between what individual Christians, local churches and different denominational or non-denominational "houses" think of as important or acceptable.

The family instruction in Romans 14 is that we should be considerate of brothers and sisters who have views which are different from ours – not to be judgemental of them (v10).

There are three areas of difference mentioned in this chapter:

- Eating or not eating meat. The similar passage in 1Corinthians 8 explains that the issue at that time was about meat which had previously been offered to idols as a sacrifice, then sold in the market.

- Treating or not treating particular days as special. This would relate to Sabbath observance and other "holy" days in a religious calendar.

- Drinking or not drinking wine (v21). Abstaining from drinking wine and other alcoholic drink was a practice associated with a person being set apart for God – either for the particular time of a vow as described in Numbers 6 v1-4, in Judges 13 for Samson's mother or for a lifetime as in Luke 1v15 – John the Baptist.

While these particular examples may not be the issues of disagreement we have with our brothers and sisters, they do point to areas where our attitudes may not be the same as one another.

The eating of meat suggests the area of "How much can or should we be involved in what might be described as worldly culture without being contaminated by it?"

The special days suggests the variety of worship practices that churches and denominations adopt that distinguishes them from others.

The wine issue suggests the decisions of personal devotion that we each make.

In each of these areas there are obvious differences of approach by individuals, local congregations and denominations and church groupings.

- We are instructed not to put down, belittle, write off brothers and sisters because they are different from us.

- We are not to be judgemental about different ways that other brothers and sisters seek to serve God.

- We are not to pull away from/dissociate with others because they have a different way of doing things.

- We are to seek to avoid deliberately doing things (which we would consider quite acceptable) but which would bring difficulties to others in their journey of faith.

Romans 14 v1 says that we are to "receive" others with differences – The words used means more than just accepting them, putting up with them, it means "taking them to yourself" – so being proactive in welcoming them and having fellowship with them (regardless of whether they might not be keen to welcome you!), and there is added the probably much needed reminder that we are not to welcome people so that we can have the opportunity to criticise their views or argue them into our way of thinking!

Verse 17 instructs us to keep our focus on what is important in God's kingdom – righteousness, peace and joy in the Holy Spirit - and to prioritise those in our lives in such a way as will build up our brothers and sisters in their faith.

CONSIDERATION IN DISPUTES

By the way that Paul writes in 1 Corinthians 6v1-8, we can feel how horrified he is at disputes in the church family being taken to the lawcourts to be decided on by non-Christians. The kind of situation where a Christian brother might have a grievance against another is mentioned in James 5v4 where payment is being withheld for work done. Rather than all the potential harm that may come from a legal dispute, if agreement cannot be reached by those involved, then they can ask for wisdom from others in the family who would be able to mediate to find a righteous resolution. Another way forward is for the person who believes that they have been wronged, to forgive what is thought to be owed, and to accept the personal loss. Perhaps the reason that some may be tempted to sue someone in the courts is because they hope for a better personally advantageous outcome than the church family will allow them!

Paul recognises that what he is advocating is a different way of life from that which is the background of many before they joined the family – and urges them to live as they should in the new family "and such were some of you, but you are washed, set apart, made right in the name of the Lord Jesus and by the Spirit of our God" (v11).

Note: These verses are in no way a justification for any criminal behaviour by members of the church family being hidden from the appropriate legal authorities. Extensive hurt and damage has been done by church authorities doing such.

CONSIDERATION IN SPEAKING

In speaking <u>about</u> brothers and sisters.

James 4v11 instructs us not to speak against brothers and sisters. The word used has the sense of speaking in such a way as to put them down. Doing such is putting ourselves in the position of the one who decides what the rules and conduct of life are and making a judgement of others who we think are not living to <u>our</u> standards. We should rather see ourselves as being alongside them as those who are also subject to Father's assessment of our behaviour.

We all have our views about how the Christian life should be lived, and others in the family will have different views. Whether or not we are right in our assessments of what others are doing, our speaking about them should be to lift them up, to build them up, not to put them down.

In speaking <u>to</u> brother and sisters

James 5v9 instructs us not to groan or moan at one another. Where the same word *stenazo* is used in a number of places (Mark7v34; Romans 8v22,23; 2 Corinthians 5v2,4), it is about expressing a deep feeling of wanting things to be different.

No doubt there are things about some brothers and sisters that we wish were different. I once heard someone usefully say in a different context, "Just because you see it, does not mean you should say it"! We are reminded that Someone who wishes that things were different in us is nearby. That should guard us from unhelpful talk.

CONSIDERATION IN RELATIONSHIPS

Respectful relationships

1 Timothy 5 verses 1 and 2 contain instructions given by Paul to Timothy, but they have a lesson for us all to apply. It begins with an instruction not to treat an older man in an aggressive way. The phrase used means – Don't lash out or don't hit out – with the intention of wounding or punishing.

Why is Timothy being told that? I presume because he was facing situations where he might be tempted to react in that way. Timothy was a young man (4v12 says he is not to let anyone look down on him because he is young), and he had a big responsibility – to teach and bring order and to correct wrong teaching in the church family at Ephesus.

Sometimes a younger person serving in the church can feel intimidated by older family members – and some older people are intimidating to younger leaders and are resistant to change. It can be tempting to get into a fight with them in order to get things done. Instead, an instruction is given using the word *parakaleo* which means "to call alongside" . In different places in the New Testament it is translated as beseech, exhort, comfort, desire, entreat, beg, plead, ask for help. It implies asking someone to do something in such a way as will encourage them and expect them to give a positive response.

In seeking to get things done which may not at first be welcomed, this is the instruction on how we should treat people with proper respect in the church family – appealing to an older man as to a father, to older women as to mothers, to young ones in the family as brothers and sisters and in all these relationships being pure in our motives and actions.

Changing relationships

1 Timothy 6v1,2

When someone becomes a Christian they might be in a relationship that they find difficult – as those in this Bible example who were in slavery, or serving a harsh master, or employed by an inconsiderate boss. There is the instruction to change what might have been a resentful attitude to one of honourable service as a testimony to the reality of the change that God has made in their lives. But then can come the added complication if their employer becomes a believer. Do they then have to be as careful about their behaviour? The instruction to them is not to "think down" or as we might say "look down" on them with the attitude, "He's just a brother so he shouldn't expect so much from me".

The Moffat Bible paraphrases verse 2 well: "Those who have Christian believers as their masters must not take liberties with them because they are brothers; they must be all the better servants because those who get the good of their service are believers and beloved."

Philemon

The letter to Philemon is for a changing relationship with instruction this time for the "employer".

Onesimus, Philemon's slave has run away. We might wonder how Philemon felt about that?

Onesimus has found his way to Rome where he met Paul who had introduced him to being a Christian. Now Onesimus is going back to his "employer" and Paul writes to smooth the way by informing Philemon that Onesimus is not coming back as his runaway servant, he is coming back as a brother. Paul instructs Philemon to receive him with love.

While we don't have any slaves who might run away and return, there may be those joining the church family who in the past have in some way offended us, taken advantage of us, or have caused us loss, financial or otherwise.

The instruction here is a good preparation for us to be ready if and when that happens to welcome them as a brother, and if we follow the inference of what Paul says, to forgive whatever they owe us. Or perhaps we might find ourselves in the place of Paul where it will be our opportunity to encourage the family to welcome unexpected new brothers and sisters.

James 1v9

James speaks of poor brothers of low status being lifted up and the rich brothers being lowered from their exalted position, now being brothers in the same family, and both rejoicing in the change.

For the poor who have been used to being looked down on, overlooked, rejected or not having enough, their new place in the church family brings them welcoming acceptance of Father and his children, being honoured as brother or sister, and benefitting from the shared resources of the family they are now part of. That is good cause to rejoice!

The rich person has something to rejoice about too. In the world, they will have had the pressure of living up to expectations of a lifestyle where so much is judged on appearance, they will have had the attention of people whose interest in them would have been to get something from them, and they will have had all the stress that acquiring riches brings. Now in the church family they can relax from all that, knowing that their new brothers and sisters have no ulterior motive in being friends with them, and also discovering the benefit of spiritual riches that far outshine material wealth.

Then in James 2v1-9 there are the instructions to make sure that there is equal acceptance of rich and poor by the family, not only those who are in the family, but also newcomers to their family gatherings.

We are not to give undue honour to the well-dressed rich, or to dishonour the scruffily dressed poor. That's easy to say, but it is more difficult to break from the worldly mindset that is so prevalent. This made me think about churches' mission statements. James 1v9 is like the "We are a church family who...." and then the instruction in James 2v1-9 is "Make sure that you do it!"

I wonder whether anything like this appears in any church's mission statement: *"We are a church family who offer no special privilege or position to anyone based on their wealth or social status, but are happy to welcome them with the same Christian love that we offer freely to all, including the poorest and most deprived in society."*

3) RESPONSIBILITY

We have already looked at the examples of leadership responsibilities in the church in Acts, and there is more in the letters about the work of those with different gifts and callings. The following examples of the prominent apostle Paul serve as instruction to those in any kind of leadership in the church in understanding their role, not as having organisational or hierarchical authority, but rather a place of service to their brothers and sisters.

1 Corinthians 12v28 states that God has set people in the church family to fulfil particular responsibilities, among them, apostles – the word meaning "one sent". Paul was not at all reticent in saying that he had that calling, introducing himself as such in most of his letters, and he could be very harsh with those who opposed, distorted or misrepresented his message. So it is informative to read how that calling was expressed in what he said about his relationship to the church families he was writing to.

- Paul described himself as a <u>partner</u> with the church family he was writing to, saying in 2 Corinthians 1v24, that he was not out to dictate to them like a lord over them in their faith, he was not interfering with their personal responsibility, but rather he was a worker together with them for them to fully experience the joy of their faith.

- Paul described himself as a <u>servant</u> of the church family he was writing to in 2 Corinthians 4v5 in contrast to their relationship with Jesus whom they should recognise and relate to as their Lord.

- Paul described himself as a <u>builder</u> in 2 Corinthians 10v8 saying that the authority he has been given as an apostle to the church family he is writing to is to be constructive, to build them up, not to pull them down or belittle them.

- Paul described himself as being like a <u>providing parent</u> in 2 Corinthians 12v14. He wanted to see them, not for anything he could get from them, but rather for fellowship with them and the opportunity to do something for them, in the way that a parent would see it as their responsibility to care for and provide for their children.

- In 1 Thessalonians 2v6-12 Paul says that when he came to this church family he was not seeking glory for himself – what we might call celebrity status - nor was he looking to be a burden to them. He did not want them feeling obliged to do things for him because he was an apostle. Instead he describes his relationship to then as being like <u>a mother</u> gently caring for her children (v7) and like <u>a father</u> with his children (v11): getting alongside them to help (the word is *parakaleo* - to call alongside); giving them reassurance (the word is *paramutheomai* – to speak alongside, to comfort as in the Jews speaking to Mary and Martha in John 11 when their brother had died); sharing with them what he knew from his personal experience (the word is *marturomai* - to testify). In describing himself in this way Paul is speaking of the quality of his loving care for them. He is not seeking to be or suggesting that he is in any kind of parental authority over them. Before, between and after these statements, Paul addresses them as "brothers".

RESPONSIBILITY QUALIFICATION

Paul writes to Timothy of the personal qualities he should look for in those who wanted to be in the work of church leadership. After giving a list of such requirements, Paul focusses on one – that church leaders should be able to manage their own family responsibilities well, and he makes the point that if they don't know how to do that, they will not be equipped for responsibility in the church family. The word that he uses for that leadership responsibility is to "take care of" God's church.

To help us know what "take care of" means, the word *epimeleomai* is used only here and in Luke 10v34,35 when it is used of the "Good Samaritan" taking care of the wounded man and what he asks the inn-keeper to continue to do at his (the Samaritan's) expense.

I imagine Timothy, having received these instructions, interviewing someone who would like to be considered for leadership in his church family.

Timothy – "Well it is a good thing to want to do; can you tell me what skills or experience you have which would make you eligible for this work?"

Well, I am very well educated…   "Sorry, that doesn't count"

I am successful in business…   "No."

I have been religious all my life.. "No that doesn't help"

I am considered to be a good employer.. "No"

I have served on the local council… "No"

I am good with financial administration… "No"

Well what is it that you are looking for?

" Tell me, how are things at home? What's your relationship with your wife and your children like?"

Well, I am rather busy…

"Mmmm"

The reason that personal family life is so important here is because Church is Family!

4) PROVISION

These next references are not so much instructions as they are a reminder of something that was fundamental from the beginning of the church family – that family resources were shared so that no one was left in need without help.

James 1v27 is a reminder of Father's priority in what he is looking for in those who are seeking to serve and worship Him. It is to look out for, to come to the help of, to target for particular care, those who are fatherless, orphans and widows, recognising the pressures, troubles and difficulties they face. This benefits them in more than one way. Along with the financial and material help that they are given, perhaps even more important is that they are brought into the additional family relationships and personal support of the church family.

Then in James 2v15-17 James uses the illustration of seeing a brother or sister without the basics in life and wishing them well without doing anything to provide for them as an example of a dead faith.

I was impressed by the action of one church I was in who, in order to help some socially deprived families, paid off completely their crippling debts to give them a fresh start, with alongside help to learn the skill of managing their finances.

5) DISCIPLINE AND CORRECTION

Exclusion

1 Corinthians 5v11 deals with someone who calls themselves a Christian brother and expects to be accepted as such by the church family, but whose behaviour is in total contradiction to the values of Jesus in such things as being: sexually immoral, greedy, idolater, slanderer, a drunkard or a swindler. It is not talking about people who have had these issues in their past, or those who may be battling to overcome aspects of them in their lives, but those who think that is acceptable to continue in that lifestyle and still be considered to be a member of the church family. The instruction is to 1) withdraw from them, not to mix with them, not to give any signals of acceptance of their lifestyle, for instance by having meals with them. 2) to exclude them from church family life. That

will mean an action which is clear to the person about what is being done and why.

Failing to do this and accepting their behaviour in the church family would pollute and disrupt family life and distort and misrepresent the message and values of the family . It would also fail to give the person a clear understanding of what it means to come into and be a member of that family. Excluding them is a loving action.

Warning

2 Thessalonians 3v6-15 deals with a different situation of discipline and it is important not to mix the two up. This is dealing with someone in the family – a brother – whose life is significantly disorderly. The example here is of someone not bothering to work and taking advantage of the family's shared provision and spending their time being a nuisance to other people – one might paraphrase what is said as "sticking their nose into other people's business while not minding their own".

The instruction is to withdraw from them, not to join them in what they are doing or to signal any acceptance of their actions. Those who are hearing this letter's instructions are to get on with working as they should to support themselves. If anyone is not responding to this message, others are instructed to withdraw from mixing with him, so that he will realise that something is wrong in the way he is behaving. But he is not to be treated as an enemy by refusing to have anything to do with him, but rather, brothers should warn him as a brother – talk to him about it, help him to understand what the issue is and what he should do about it.

6) INTEGRITY

An important theme in 1 John is the importance of integrity in the relationships in the church family. John sets the scene by saying that God is Light and there is no darkness in Him. He says that if we say that we share life with God, but our lifestyle is that of darkness, then we are lying and don't have a grasp on truth (1v6). He goes on to say that one aspect of a darkness lifestyle is when someone, while professing to live in the Light - hates his brother (2v9), and that if he says that he loves God but hates his brother, then he is a liar (4v20).

The word "hate" in the New Testament is used as we would normally use it, but also to disregard someone for the sake of choosing someone else, so it could cover when we give preferential treatment to one brother at the expense of being equally considerate of another.

But the matter of integrity goes further than simply not being negative about someone else in the family. 1 John 3v10 says that you can see who are God's children in contrast to the devil's children. One of the ways is that someone who does not love his brother does not belong to God. Professed love will be seen in practical compassionate care and support in providing for a brother's needs, or there will be no credibility that he is letting God's love influence his life (4v20).

It is worth reminding ourselves that our brothers and sisters are not only those who, like us, have decided to be part of the same local congregation of God's family (however challenging we might find that!) but also brothers and sisters very different from ourselves in other churches, denominations, social backgrounds, cultures in other places across the world. The instruction about integrity applies to our attitude and actions relating to all.

4. FAMILY GATHERINGS

Before looking at the description and instructions concerning church family gatherings in the letters, it is important to see that there were different kinds of such gatherings which are mentioned in Acts.

1) FAMILY GATHERINGS IN ACTS

PRAYER

The first meetings of the church family were for **prayer** as they waited for the promised outpouring of the Holy Spirit (Acts 1v14).

When, following the healing of the lame man at the temple, Peter and John had been arrested and then released, there was a gathering for prayer (4v23-31).

When the apostle James had been killed and Peter had been arrested and imprisoned, there was a prayer meeting of many people (12v12).

HOLY SPIRIT EMPOWERED EVANGELISM

The gathering of the church family in Acts 2 resulted in **Holy Spirit empowered evangelism** which was felt and heard by the surrounding community leading to 3000 joining the church family.

PUBLIC GATHERINGS

The church family had **public gatherings** in the temple courtyard. Acts 5v12 mentions that they met in Solomon's Porch which was where Jesus has answered questions from Jews who had engaged him in conversation (John 10v23). While it does not describe all that the church family did there, the verse begins with the apostles being used in signs and wonders among the people, and afterwards it states that the church family was a distinct recognisable group in that public area.

MEETINGS FOR CHURCH FAMILY BUSINESS

There were **meetings for church family business**. There was a meeting to organise the management of distribution of resources (Acts 6v2-6), and a gathering to find an agreed answer and strategy concerning a doctrinal dispute (Acts 15).

TEACHING MEETINGS

In Antioch, Barnabas and Saul met with the church family in Antioch for a year of well- attended **teaching meetings** (Acts 11v26).

FELLOWSHIP MEETING

There is the account in Acts 20v7-12 of the church family at Troas meeting "to break bread". Whether we think of this as meaning having a fellowship meal together, or sharing in "the Lord's Supper", it covers both as we will see in 1Corinthians 11 where the two go together on the same occasion. But this **fellowship meeting** was even more than that. Paul made use of the opportunity as he was about to leave them the next day, and he did a lot of talking. The word used *dialegomai* (v7) means that he discussed with them – it was a conversational teaching time. After the interruption of raising a young man back from the dead, there followed continued conversation until daybreak.

MISSIONARY FAREWELL MEETING

Acts 21v5,6 describes what I would call a **missionary farewell meeting** – all ages of the church family at Tyre giving Paul's missionary team a good prayerful send-off as they boarded ship to continue their journey.

2) FAMILY GATHERINGS IN THE LETTERS

PRAYER

Although the instructions in 1 Timothy 2 do not refer specifically to church family gatherings, they are certainly relevant to them, and show that the church family's concern in prayer is not only about themselves but is outward-looking to the needs of everyone in society. A study of the different words used in 1Timothy 2v1 suggests:

- We are asking because we and others have a <u>need</u>. Supplications/requests – {*deesis* - having regard to our necessity}

- We are asking because God has the <u>power</u> to meet those needs. Prayers – {*proseuche* - having regard to the power of Him who is asked}

- We are asking because we have the <u>relationship</u> with God which allows us to ask. Intercession – {*enteuxis* - confiding access to God giving prominence to childlike confidence in prayer}

- We are asking because God will <u>answer</u>, and the prayer is focussed on seeking conditions to be such that it is easy for anyone to come to know the truth of Jesus as Saviour. Thanksgiving – {*eucharistia* - thankfulness}

FELLOWSHIP MEAL AND THE LORD'S SUPPER

When Jesus shared the first "Lord's Supper" as it is called in 1 Corinthians 11, it was at the end of a meal with his disciples. The church at Corinth continued that practice as described in 11v18-34. The fellowship meal would have had the food and drinks which each person brought. Some richer people were bringing plenty for themselves but ignoring the needs of poorer brothers and sisters. They were selfishly overindulging. This meant that they were missing the point of this family gathering. When they were joining in "the Lord's Supper", what they were signifying by participating was contradicted by their inappropriate selfish behaviour.

The corrective instruction given in verse 34 that if someone was hungry, he should eat at home, was to indicate that this family gathering was not for personal enjoyment of food and drink, but for fellowship with brothers and sisters and Jesus as they ate together. On such an occasion they should be looking out for one another, not themselves. It is made clear that participating wrongly in an act of fellowship with brothers and sisters meant that one is participating wrongly in any act of fellowship with Jesus, and such presumptuous action can lead to severe Fatherly discipline.

The simplicity of what is instructed about the Lord's Supper in the words of verses 23-29 has been taken in a considerable variety of directions by churches and denominations, so that the way it is practised is sometimes difficult to connect with the family gathering we read of here. This is not to say that things cannot be added to a time of sharing the Lord's Supper. In Acts 20v7-12, Paul added an all-night discussion/teaching/conversation!

When there are so many variations practised on the theme of what is meant to be a family gathering, it is important to recognise the heart of what is intended – people whose lives have been changed by Jesus demonstrating loving togetherness with one another, their brothers and sisters, and together demonstrating their personal and family togetherness with and commitment to Jesus.

Whatever add-on practices we may adopt, our family gatherings which include the Lord's Supper should be measured in how well they are a true expression of that.

AN OVERFLOW GATHERING

The church in Corinth were very enthusiastic in experiencing and expressing the Holy Spirit gifts they had received. In 1 Corinthians 14 Paul gives them some guidance for their family gatherings which were characterised by an abundant overflow of these gifts. Paul encourages their enthusiasm but gives a corrective to their overconcentration on the gift of tongues to the neglect of the other gifts, and also helps them to understand that some of their personal expressions of worship, while being perfectly valid in themselves, may at times be not best suited to the family gathering.

While Paul's teaching and instructions are particularly for the Corinthian church family, there are lessons we can learn from their example, and some instructions which can be applied to our church family gatherings. The family came together to share together the overflow of their experiences of the Holy Spirit. It was a gathering which was open to many people participating and contributing.

Participation is to come from a flow of love not just from an experience or gift that the Holy Spirit has given (1Cor 13. 2). Rather than being enthusiastic to use the gifts, our enthusiasm should be about the opportunity to strengthen the church family (14v12,31). All that is being done should in some way further the purpose of building up the church, and to be easily understood and appreciated even by unbelieving visitors (14v16,23,24). Participants are expected to exercise self-control in their own participation (14v28), in giving way to one another's participation(v30), and in avoiding unnecessary conversation that is more appropriate for another time (v35).

The instruction in verses 34,35 for women or wives to be silent in the gathering appears to refer to inappropriate talking rather than a ban on them participating. Whatever particular cultural issues are involved, we have to see Paul's instruction here alongside what he said earlier in 1 Corinthians 11v5, about an inappropriate way in which a woman might pray or prophesy in a gathering – and a similar observation about men's participation – showing that there are appropriate ways for both men and women to participate in their use of Holy Spirit gifts. (Acts 2v17,18 includes children too). And Paul observes that all may share God's message (prophesy) for everyone to learn and be encouraged (14v31).

It is worth noting that the instruction in verse 40 - that "everything should be done decently and in order" – is not to stop an enthusiastic overflow of Holy Spirt gifts, but to welcome them and manage a family gathering where so many people have something they would like to contribute, that some guidelines are needed to show consideration to one another.

MUSIC GATHERINGS

In Ephesians 5v18-21 and Colossians 3v16-17, Paul encourages the church family to have gatherings when they sing together. In the introduction to these times he encourages them to go on being filled with the Holy Spirit (Ephesians 5v18) and to let Jesus' words be so at home in their hearts that they will have the wisdom to help one another (Colossians 3v16).

He mentions a variety of songs and music:

- **psalms** – which indicate songs of happy rejoicing – as in James 5v13 –"Is anyone happy? Let him "psalm" - and

Romans 15v9,10. The word "psalm" comes from a word which associates it with playing a stringed instrument.

- **hymns** – songs of praise – like Paul and Silas in prison Acts 16v25.

- **spiritual songs** – the word for song here is used in Revelation 5v9 and 15v3 of songs declaring the truth about Jesus. Spiritual songs could include songs inspired by the Holy Spirit, songs on a spiritual theme, or songs using the gift of tongues as Paul mentions in 1 Corinthians 14v15.

- **singing and "making music"** in/with your hearts (Ephesians 5v19). This does not mean something that is not outwardly expressed, but rather singing "heartily" as an expression of what is in your heart, and/or it could mean composing songs and music, as the Old Testament Psalm's encouragement to "sing a new song to the Lord"(Psalm 96v1).

Both passages in Ephesians and Colossians end by saying that all this should be done in the context of thanksgiving with the focus on Jesus.

ALL FAMILY GATHERINGS

Appropriate for all the various church family gatherings, Peter in his letter has instructions which cover them all beautifully (1 Peter 4v8-11)

Above everything, loving each other deeply because love covers a multitude of sins.

Offering hospitality to one another without grumbling.

Using whatever gift we have received to serve others.

Faithfully administering God's grace in its various forms.

If speaking, then doing it as one speaking the words of God.

If serving, doing it with the strength that God provides.

Doing all those things so that God will be praised through Jesus Christ.

CHALLENGE AND ENCOURAGEMENT

That completes our exploration of "Church is Family" in the New Testament.

On several occasions after I have preached, someone has said, "We thank Graeme for that challenging word", and I have thought, "What was challenging about it? I was doing my best to be positively encouraging!". Then I wondered if their definition of a challenging word, was one that they were not prepared to doing anything about at the moment!

I recognise, however, that along with the encouragements in this study, there is plenty to challenge us all. As you consider your own response, you might be encouraged, enjoy and be inspired by some of the "Church is Family" familiness that I have had the privilege of experiencing in different parts of Jesus' family. These examples show, that although the denominational structures and organisation that are adopted by churches do not always clearly represent church as family, in all sorts of churches, "Church is Family" finds expression.

CHURCH IS FAMILY
IN MY EXPERIENCE

ALBERT STREET LANE GOSPEL HALL, FRASERBURGH

The first church in my memory is Albert Street Lane Gospel Hall in Fraserburgh which I attended from 1953-58 when I was 3 to 8 years old. I particularly remember two married couples – Annabella and Gilbert Duthie – Annabella, a vivacious woman, and her much quieter husband, Gilbert. Then a gentle ever-smiling older couple, Alec and Mary Tait.

Why do I remember them? Because as a family we would be invited to their homes after the Sunday evening Gospel meeting – and that happened often enough for me to remember them more than others with whom we did not have that hospitality relationship.

My Sunday school teacher, James Sutherland, who would have been a teenager at that time is special to me. A lesson he taught me about the meaning of saving faith from the story of Moses holding up the bronze snake on the pole has stayed with me ever since. This church family connection was renewed about 40 years later in a day's hill walking together, after which he was able to tell me the exact date he had taught me that lesson as he still had all his notes of that time!

ASSEMBLY HALL, PORTESSIE

The year after my father died as the result of an accident at work, we moved back to my mother's family home in Portessie. The (Brethren) Assembly Hall (or "the Meetin" as it was commonly called) was not only my next church but the place where I gave my life to Jesus on September 20th 1959 – aged nine.

There was the familiness there of human family ties with a good number of the congregation being my mother's cousins and their families. A highlight stemming from these relationships (along with a weekly Sunday supply of sweets!) was the "Pan Loafie Picnic" – an all-age outing along the coast to a sheltered bay which had a loaf-shaped rock, the seashore and a cave to explore. Everything for the picnic had to be carried the mile or so – kettles were boiled on an open camp-fire – games with all ages joining in for this Kingdom of heaven family time! It was interesting to discover many years later that my mother's cousins, Kate and Janet had come up with the idea of this event to coincide with the weekend of the annual local "Peter Fair" – in order to provide families with a more wholesome enjoyable alternative.

Portessie was another place of Sunday evening church hospitality. Sometimes we would walk the mile to "Major's" house in Findochty, but more often we would be at "Auntie Elsie's" (not our aunt!) conveniently situated a few doors from the meeting hall. These occasions of fellowship always included a wonderful selection of things to eat, so us children had plenty to enjoy and were not excluded. Years later, in thinking back to that time, I realised how important to me had been the friendship of Auntie Elsie's son-in-law, Billy Gault. On these evenings, when I was nine of ten years old, and he was "old" (probably about thirty!) he spent time with me personally as a friend, and I believe that sharing those short times together managed to cover in a significant way the gap of relationship that had been left by the absence of my Dad. It was good to meet Billy many years later to thank him, and the familiness of that time continued to be expressed for many more years when I have received an annual Christmas card from his wife, Jessie.

BUCKIE BAPTIST CHURCH

When I was about 13 years old, I moved to join my brother, James at Buckie Baptist church – a church family where young people were given our full place. We were encouraged – and *expected* to participate – whether in Christian Endeavour, Youth Fellowship meetings, singing in services, Sunday school teaching, and even "street fishing" to invite unsuspecting local youths and others to come and join us for some special evangelistic event.

Looking back I have identified something that was special in the church's familiness which I must have taken for granted at the time. It was that there was no "generation-gap". We all seemed to know and talk to one another regardless of age. People were interested and appreciative of one another and friendships spanned the age groups.

A particular expression of Buckie Baptist Church's familiness was demonstrated by two people in particular. The minister, Mr Barr was a good example of something that I have since taught – "If God has put you in leadership in the church, then he has made you a minister to the community." When families in Buckie hit crises, they knew who they could call on, whether or not they had any church connection. Mr Barr would be there to help them through their difficult times.

The other person was my mother. She always had a heart for people in need, and particularly in times of bereavement, she would assemble the best of the baker's and/or her own baking and deliver it as her gift of love. Such ministry lasts a long time in its effect. In recent years I have met a man who was much affected when many years ago, on the morning after he heard of his daughter's death, my mum was at the door with rolls and other provisions to save them having to think of shopping when they had so much else to deal with. The preciousness of that expression of familiness still lives with that old man.

One other familiness expression there was from my brother, James. I was sixteen and was being baptised (James was eighteen at the time). James walked alongside me to the baptismal pool and held my hand as I was about to go into the water. I don't suppose we had held hands with one another for about ten years, and there was something very special and memorable in that way of standing alongside me as my Christian brother in the step I was taking.

Before moving on from the north east of Scotland, I want to mention Sunday school picnics. They were great church family times - not just children's events. Buses and cars would head off for a park or recreation ground when togetherness was expressed in a variety of ways – the boys and men would play football together while the women and girls might concentrate on skipping with a huge rope (men and boys sometimes joining in). All manner of races would be run and games with bats and balls would be enjoyed. Ice-cream would be supplied and a bag of "pieces" – such as sandwich, chocolate biscuit and cream cookie for our picnic tea.

Jumping forward to my years in England, I was very disappointed to find that in various churches there, the idea of a Sunday school outing was to take everyone to a theme park or the seaside, let them off the coach to go and spend the afternoon as they chose, then take them home again. I enjoyed organising for south east Londoners the experience of a re-created north east of Scotland picnic. I asked (required) each of the 10 congregations in the Ichthus East area church for a set amount of money so that the event had all the right ingredients including no charge for anyone attending. For the wide range of family backgrounds of the inner-city children, young people and adults, I expect it meant even more to them than my childhood experiences meant to me.

ARBURY ROAD BAPTIST CHURCH, CAMBRIDGE

When I was seventeen I moved to Cambridge to live with my sister and to work there. I expected to find a place in the church family of the Baptist Church, only to find that there were six to choose from!

I was attracted to one which had its own familiness expression in its "all-age Sunday school" – a type of structure that I had seen once on a visit to Gillingham Baptist Church which my brother, Ian attended. In the service, all ages met together, then split for their group times when adults had Bible study discussion, and the whole church met together at the end.

Inconveniently, Arbury Road Baptist Church was on the opposite side of Cambridge to where I was living, but it was worth it! At the end of the first service I attended, Brian the youth pastor welcomed me and introduced me to John, who, like me had recently come to find work in Cambridge. We were friends or should I say, brothers from that day, having long conversations putting the world to right, serving together as officers in the Boys Brigade, sharing in the life of the youth fellowship and working together in the church's evangelistic youth club.

I hope that Brian and his wife Jean intended to have an "open home" because I certainly took advantage of it, and treated their house as a home from home. It was great to have a friendly home I could go to at any time, to share in their family life and ministry, and times of joys and sorrows – theirs and mine. Their friendship and encouragement to me to pursue God's calling on my life was a blessing, and that home was a place of nurture for our group of young people who grew numerically and spiritually.

CAMBRIDGE CHRISTIAN YOUNG PEOPLE

The 1970s saw a widespread and fruitful familiness among Christian young people in Cambridge. Krystyna saw a group handing out political leaflets as people passed through Drummer Street Bus station and had the idea/vision of distributing evangelistic leaflets when young people passed through on their way home from school. She mentioned the idea to her boyfriend, John who was a recent convert in my young people's group, and he asked for my help in writing suitable material. Thus began "Jesus and Co. Unlimited". In our first hour, six young people from two churches handed out 1000 leaflets. Within a few weeks of these Thursday distributions, we had grown to twenty from six churches – and made Jesus and our leaflets the common topic of conversations in the local secondary schools.

That group continued and took to the streets of the city centre occasionally to sing and evangelise tourists and shoppers, then formed the core of the Jesus Tent team at the annual Cambridge Folk Festival weekend throughout that decade.

The Christian family grew among the schools. Nineteen secondary schools in and around Cambridge had active Christian groups in them at that time.

There has been long-term fruitfulness in the lives of those who shared in the original "Jesus and Co" familiness. I don't know what has happened to them all, but I have discovered that one of them has had many years of church leadership, been a director of mission and pastoral studies, been in charge of a number of parishes, co-authored a book on evangelism and has been carrying responsibility as "change officer" in his diocese to bring in a range of new congregations and fresh expressions of church.

Another has served as a missionary, pastor and church planter and director of ministry for a national church organisation.

John and Krystyna, the initiators of the vision later got married and have continued to serve Jesus – most recently in leadership in the work of Africa Inland Mission in Uganda.

There is another long-lasting and very personal result of that small beginning in "Jesus and Co. Unlimited". At the first prayer meeting before going out on the streets, fourteen year old Katy saw and liked the leather-jacketed youth leader leading the meeting. She married him four years later, and we are another example of the fruit of what was begun at that time.

The familiness of young people of the churches across Cambridge was added to by the love and support shown to us by older leaders. When John and I sent out information about the beginning of "Jesus and Co. Unlimited", Canon Mark Ruston of the Round Church invited us for tea and encouraged us. Peter Phenna of St Martins Church gave us a place to meet, and printed our leaflets – and arranged for the Cambridge Evangelical Association to pay for them and to give us ongoing support and fellowship in our ministry at the Folk Festival. That familiness across the churches was to me a special place of belonging. Arranging the Cambridge Easter Dawn service and involvement in the city and area wide evangelistic Christian Festival with evangelist David Watson were particular privileges.

QUEEN EDITH CHAPEL (named after the local area!), CAMBRIDGE

In 1973 I moved from Arbury Road Baptist church to Queen Edith Chapel – as Mr Walder, one of the elders described it – "Christian brethren with a capital C and a small b!" Familiness was increased there by the introduction of family services and housegroups.

The familiness among the young people in Austin and Betty's home (and in later years in Donovan and Rosemary's and our own) was such that it attracted others who were befriended and added to Jesus' family. It was not an inward-looking familiness. One girl from St Matthew's Church lacked the blessing of a young people's group in her own church, so asked if she could come to our youth fellowship and bring her friends there to begin with. When enough of her friends had been nurtured in our group, they left us to plant that group in their own church.

A precious expression of familiness at QEC was one that I think few knew about. Once, we were in conversation with a couple who had been there from the beginning of the church and who were, as we were, renting a council house. They mentioned that when the building was being built, funded by the members of that time, they had money which they had intended to use to buy a house for themselves and their children. Instead, they donated it to help in the establishing of the church and contented themselves to continue in their rented house.

An important incident of familiness happened following a church business meeting. I had introduced a subject to be considered, and in frustration at something the chairman said, I reacted with a comment which was dishonouring to him and frankly quite rude! I knew I had done wrong but did not know what to do about it. At the end of the meeting, Austin came and sat beside me, gently told me that I needed to put things right and accompanied me to David's house to apologise – and be forgiven! That brotherly help mended the relationship, and when I moved to work with another church, it was David who came and preached at my introduction there.

SHERIDAN ROAD EVANGELICAL CHURCH, BELVEDERE
(south east London)

I carried to Belvedere my openness and desire to have fellowship with people from different churches, the value and blessing of which I had been introduced to in my years in Cambridge. The first "test" of this resolve came shortly after we arrived. A leaflet came through the letterbox advertising special meetings at the local Pentecostal church. That was a setting I had not previously experienced and I had my preconceived ideas/worries? about what such a meeting might include. I had this conversation with myself – "Graeme, do you feel threatened by attending? If you don't, then there is no reason why you should not go. If you do, then there is all the more reason why you must go!"

I went, and after the first lively hymn, which the men on the platform were clearly enjoying, the pastor (who I had met just once before) welcomed everyone, and then said, "Graeme, would you please begin our meeting by leading us to the Lord in prayer". I barely had time to recover from this unexpected expression of familiness when a little later, he invited me to the platform to share with the congregation how I had come to know Jesus.

In our small fellowship, we decided to share our familiness with the surrounding community by delivering to 1000 homes a monthly church family newsletter. This was intended to be part of a long-term relationship building exercise, in which it was a success, but as a direct result of the first newsletter five new children came to our Monday night club, George attended our "Family Time" service for the first time and came regularly from then on, I had a phone call from Frank, and a new young mum came to the Thursday club. Also, some weeks later, Violet, because she saw our name, contact details and offer of personal and practical help on the leaflet, decided to call us and receive support and the church's friendship rather go through with suicide which she had been contemplating. Clearly some in the community were simply waiting for an expression of familiness to come to them.

LUIS PALAU MISSION TO LONDON

Familiness can have unusual connections. Syd and Vi Ray from Plumstead, south east London took their holidays in Portessie and were friends with my mother, her cousins and others in the brethren assembly. With me then living nearby, they invited me to preach on several occasions at Richmond Hall (brethren) in Plumstead.

Plans were being considered for a Luis Palau Mission to London and there was an introductory meeting for the south east area being held in Blackheath. I attended and sat at the back of the meeting of about 200 people among whom I did not see anyone I knew. Towards the end of the meeting, the chairman asked for suggestions of people who could be asked to form the executive committee for the seventeen day south east London part of the Mission. I listened while names unknown to me were mentioned and noted, and then, to my complete shock, someone whose voice I did not recognise called out, "Graeme Young from Belvedere". I discovered later that it was a member of the Richmond Hall congregation, and as a result I found myself on the executive committee which led to me carrying a number of major responsibilities in the Mission. The relationships formed there was the means of linking me to my next church family.

ICHTHUS CHRISTIAN FELLOWSHIP

Familiness in Ichthus Christian Fellowship was planned with Sunday morning family services designed to have a Jesus-focussed "magazine" style of various ingredients on a Bible theme suitable for all ages and stages.

I was told that one expression of familiness came about "by accident". When the church was just one congregation, they used the building of a German church for their services. However the German church used the building on one Sunday each month, so Ichthus, not having a congregational venue for that day, decided to meet in house-groups. (house-groups for adults were held regularly on a weeknight evening). Those monthly Sunday house-groups were informal times with children, young people and adults, worshipping, praying and learning together, and then enjoying lunch and fun and conversation. These were such a blessing that monthly Sunday house-groups became the pattern for further congregations that were planted, and came to be seen as an important statement about the nature of church.

My years in Ichthus were the setting where the understanding and practice grew that "church is family" means that the place of children in that family should be an expression of that truth. This became a central focus of my ministry. The spiritual experiences of children from that time can be read about in "Children and the Holy Spirit" (the text of my book-"Spying out the Land"). The teaching and practice developed in that time relating to children in the church family is in my Children's Ministry Manual. Both of these can be found on www.youngresources.co.uk.

We moved from any idea that children are just a group to be taught (for seeds to be sown which would not bear fruit until adulthood) to realise that children are as much part of church family as they are of their natural family – that they can know their heavenly Father as they know their earthly father, and that spiritual gifts, callings and service in the church family are not the exclusive domain of adults but are as much the area of privilege and responsibility for children to participate in.

There was a movement from doing good things *for* children and good things *with* children to being alongside good things being done *by* children. Familiness was enriched immensely by the pictures/visions and words and insights that children shared and by their prayer ministry for and alongside adults, and their partnership in leadership of discipleship and evangelistic activities for children.

Nine year old Sarah mentioned that she would like to preach at church, so when Ewen (children's work co-ordinator in the Deptford Park Congregation) heard this, he took action. On a Sunday when he was booked as the preacher, he gave the place to

Sarah instead. To prepare, Ewen met with Sarah with the Bible passage that was allocated for the day. Sarah chose the part of the passage she wanted to preach on, then they looked over it and prayed. As they talked about it together, Ewen wrote some notes on what Sarah was saying, and then gave her those notes to look at. Sarah decided most of what she wanted to say, and then Ewen wrote out what she was saying and left it with her. Sarah then wrote her own notes, and at Ewen's suggestion, thought about pictures to illustrate the points, and real life examples. At the Sunday family service, with adults and children there, Sarah preached while Ewen held up the visual aids at the appropriate times. Afterwards they together prayed for people who responded in relation to what she had just said.

She had another opportunity to preach with Ewen's help, and then with Sue's help she preached at Popcorn Children's Church to about 150 children, and when she was ten, at Target Children's Church summer camp to about 50 children. (extract from "Children and the Holy Spirit – Spying out the Land")

MUSTARD TREE CHRISTIAN FELLOWSHIP

When I and Kate moved to serve "Mustard Tree" – an Ichthus congregation, we came into a family which had been "born" a few years previously and which had been well-nurtured. During our few years there, there were about 80 plus in the congregation (at one count, 13 different nationalities) which kept changing due to additions to the family and the never-ending comings and goings which are so common in London life. One measure of the health of a family is what the members do outside the family setting. Jesus said, "Did you not know that I had to be about my Father's business?"

Among the congregation were those who at that time or soon after included: (in no particular order) a hospice staff worker, a borough voluntary work coordinator, a secondary school teacher, a borough carers' co-ordinator, a primary school teacher – who became the congregation leader, a famine relief worker, the leader, some years later of Habitat for Humanity, Northern Ireland, a missionary to Albania, a specialist AIDS nurse, a volunteer for a charity for AIDS affected families, a probation officer, a singer/musician/evangelist, two Youth with a Mission workers, a youth club leader, a famine relief charity photographer, a missionary nurse, a couple who went as missionaries to France, two people working with people with cognitive impairments, one person who went on to be an Anglican minister, another who became the children's co-ordinator of a major London church, and another who became Alpha co-ordinator in another English city – and not forgetting the children who became part of the team running "Popcorn Children's Church". We even had a "tax-collector" who like his Biblical counterpart, provided feasts for his friends on house-group Sundays! – and also took a mission team to Romania. It was a great blessing to me to be in the familiness of such a congregation before I moved to concentrate on children's ministry.

CHILDPRAYER

In London, when Chris Perkins and a few friends decided that it would be good if people who had a concern for praying for children (like them) could meet to pray with and for people who were working with children (like me), Childprayer was born. It was clear that often those involved in children's ministry were isolated from the interest, the family support structures and relationships that adults' ministry received in the churches.

Childprayer during the 1990s offered the familiness of prayer and fellowship support to people in a wide variety of ministries, and offered intercessors the opportunity to pray for known workers and situations. Along with the very valuable support and encouragement I received from the Childprayer "family", we stood alongside and prayed with and for friends in quite a number of significant ministries and projects – among them people involved in church based children's work, schools ministry, radio, literature, pastoral care, major family conferences, prayer ministry, discipleship programmes, training in the UK and overseas.

This kind of family togetherness was so fruitful that I incorporated it into the regular meetings I held for Ichthus congregations children's leaders. I invited some intercessors to meet with us at the beginning of our meeting to see who was there and what was on our agenda. They would then go to another room to pray, while we continued with our business. At a break during the evening, and at the end of the meeting, the pray-ers would return and talk with and pray with and for individuals to support and bless them – which it did!

ST MARY'S EPISCOPAL CHURCH, INVERURIE

Having grown in my commitment and experience of relating to all God's family, regardless of denominational or non-denominational label, I found that when we moved to Scotland in 1997, we were welcomed and wanted in an Episcopal church – (St Mary's in Inverurie) a new and very different setting for me!

Our relationship with that congregation came as a result of their valuing of children, and their recognition of the place of children in the church family. This made room for children's creative contribution in worship, and my own children benefitted from being part of the familiness there.

To try to fit together the various expectations and requirements of services with a desire for all-age involvement, the church experimented with different types of service on particular Sundays each month.

After our time there, I was impressed that they found a pattern which suited their situation and gave flexibility for people to fit in with whatever part or parts of the church's family life was right for them and their family. Their Sunday pattern was: 8:30am: Traditional Early Communion. 9:15am: Breakfast in the Centre. 10:00am: Young Church in the Centre, Adult Teaching in Church. 11:00am: Family Communion with All Age Talk.

This gave everyone the choice of how and when to be involved in the church's family relationships.

PRAY FOR SCOTLAND

From a church family relationship of Roger Mitchell in London with David and Jean Black in Scotland, came my connection to "Pray for Scotland" – a ministry through which David and Jean succeeded in facilitating a family togetherness across churches, denominations, streams, organisations, groups, ministries and individuals in Scotland. It was a great joy of my time as project co-ordinator to pick up an idea/vision that someone had of "Mending the Nets" (of the broken and damaged relationships of the church) a focus for prayer and action. We produced material that churches could use and sent a letter and the leaflet to every congregation in Scotland that we could find information on (about 4000 of them). In expressing fellowship in this way, I had come a long way from the much narrower view that I had grown up with, and I was particularly blessed by the letters we received in response from representatives of God's family who would not normally have much connection with one another.

Saying "sorry" is an indispensable ingredient of family life – and "Mending the Nets" suggested ways of doing that in the various church family relationships. When sharing the plans with a group we were looking to for support and involvement, I was surprised to find that several did not agree with and opposed one suggestion which was for churches to say sorry to the community for any way in which church had failed them. Several years later, however, one of that group shared how he had discovered how powerful such an expression can be. He had been with a church in Glasgow who had been on the streets to talk and pray with people and who were offering prayer (I think on a card they were handing out) and saying sorry to anyone who had been hurt, damaged or let down by their contact with church in the past. He told how when one young man was given the card and read it , he immediately burst into tears and was deeply appreciative of the expression of apology on behalf of God's family.

ST COMBS COMMUNITY CHURCH

A connection through a Christian family conference led to my involvement with St Combs Community Church. The newly planted congregation, meeting in a school hall, had these expressions of familiness. There was a break for a cup of tea and something to eat in the middle of the service, after which the preacher had his time to speak. It was such a simple activity, but one which led to a more traditional local churchgoer to judge that it "could not be a proper church"!

After the service the congregation moved to the community hall to enjoy lunch together, sometimes made and provided by members of the congregation, then by arrangement with the local shop who supplied us with fish and chips to order! Following lunch, conversations continued while a game of football in the park involved the energetic ones of various ages. These times gave lots of opportunities for relationships to be much more than just "going to church" and gave newcomers and visitors the familiness into which to come and grow in the life of the church.

STRICHEN PARISH CHURCH

Following our time there, I was involved in a planned week of prayer-walking and prayer events around the north east corner of Scotland. Following an initial meeting with church leaders at which I outlined the plan, I had a call from a minister whom I did not know previously, and he said, "If you want a place for a meeting in our area, you can use our hall." I thought, "I like this man!" He prayer-walked with us in his rural parish, and we did have a meeting there with 32 present from 13 different communities. That initial expression of familiness led us to be part of his congregation.

A small congregation scattered among the many pews of a large traditional Church of Scotland building is not the easiest setting for familiness, but Harold, one of the elders demonstrated it when he introduced a service. He gave a proper welcome to the visiting preacher, acknowledged the children, then in giving information about upcoming events, he said that one of the two young leaders of the youth group had given a report that week on their work to the church leadership. He mentioned them by name and commended them for the important work they were doing. At the end of the service he took time to thank the preacher, the keyboard player and singers, and the Boys Brigade lad who was volunteering with stewarding duties; and his invitation to tea/coffee friendship and reflection in the hall was warm and sincere. It struck me how the mentioning of people's names and valuing the contribution of each was such a simple and effective expression of familiness.

More recently, familiness is growing and being shared with the community through the weekly community café (with free refreshments) attracting all ages, and the "Sharing Larder" providing food to those who need it.

FAMILY SUPPORT

In thinking over the familiness I have experienced in all the different churches, something else came to mind which spans many years and settings of my ministry , and that is the familiness I and my family have experienced through the giving of those who have financially supported my ministry – I couldn't have done it without them!

Of five cars which took me about half a million miles, two were the generosity of family members, then someone who wanted to give a car to someone in Christian ministry and was put in touch with me, then a friend in our congregation, and then "Anonymous"!

We have many stories that could be told of the timely one-off gifts and the regular dependable support, which from some lasted many years, and have been expressions of familiness which have been very precious, fruitful and appreciated.

MEN'S BREAKFASTS

A place, or rather places of continuing familiness to me over more than 20 years in Scotland has been regular Saturday morning men's breakfasts.

Firstly in Inverurie where they were held weekly, then in Ellon and Portsoy where there have been monthly get-togethers of Christian brothers from a good mixture of churches in a wide area.

Each has had its own "style" both in the breakfast ingredients and the accompanying time together. Conversation over breakfast is truly "family" – there is no limit to the range of mundane or crucial subjects and issues that might arise! Then the focussing of hearts in singing, praying, sharing personal, family, church and other concerns, and in Portsoy, listening to a speaker.

Meeting together regularly in this way over a long time develops an understanding of one another – we are quite different from each other in many ways – and has led to a non-demanding and freely offered fellowship and mutual support which provides encouragement wherever it is needed, and has been recognised by quite a number as an important factor in the growth of their personal Christian faith, and by others as a much needed strength through difficult times.

THE LIGHTHOUSE

Along with all the familiness I have benefitted from in different churches, one setting has become an ongoing source of delight to me.

"The Lighthouse" – is a regular evening in Buckie facilitated with a light touch by my brother, James and his wife, Anne, where adults with various aspects of cognitive impairment participate in worship, teaching, prayer, craft activities, food and friendship, along with a group of helpers and accompanying support staff. The specialness of this time is the input of those who come; what happens is not being done for them, but rather by them and with them. We number in all a "congregation" of about 40.

A visiting care worker who was used to leading programmes in another town said that he had never seen anything like it. His comparison with his own situation went along the lines of:

"We spend our time doing things for them and telling them what to do. But here you've turned the whole thing upside down. It's them that do it – and you just stand back and see what they're doing."

The evening is marked by an informal orderliness or orderly informality!

Elaine likes to give a welcome to all and will add a personal comment each time especially to say something nice to any newcomers. Singing is a large part. Various members of the group have different particular worship songs which are special to them, and they will come to the microphone to lead "their song", after which they are sure to be thanked and encouraged by others. I was surprised and much blessed when I first said a prayer, and was then greeted with, "Thank you, Graeme, that was a good prayer!" (much nicer than "amen").

Without any guidance being given, although generally there might be quite a lot of interjections (all positive!) during the evening, when one is doing the Bible reading or is praying, there is complete silence.

As James once pointed out, it is a great place to be as there is a complete lack of criticism of anyone's contribution. While it is generally a very happy time, sorrows are shared and sympathy shown in conversation and in prayer.

In the time that I have been attending, I have enjoyed and been blessed by the flow of the unique personal expressions of spiritual awareness and receptivity – and also the social growth of us all in the reality of the song we sing:

"We are here together, you, and you and me,

We are brothers and sisters, one big family."

And James pointed out to me that is was those attending who began to talk of the Lighthouse family as part of God's family. Along with so much else that happens, it is evident when Mark raises his hand and leads the singing of, "As we are gathered, Jesus is here", cognitive impairment does not signify spiritual impairment!

One special aspect of this familiness is seeing its effect on the support staff who bring the members there as part of their "work". They are welcomed and gradually get used to and join in this unusual Christian family setting. It is good to watch the encouragement they get from seeing those they support in their home, taking part in the evening in special ways which they might not be expecting from their previous knowledge of them.

There are often unexpected and blessed contributions, like from one nicknamed, "the Encourager". When Anne said at the beginning of one year, "It says in the Bible that God has plans for me," his entirely appropriate response was, "Congratulations, Anne!"

If only every church was more like the Lighthouse…

AND THEN CAME CORONAVIRUS

The coronavirus pandemic with its resultant shutdown of people meeting together posed quite a challenge for churches whose main activities involve meeting together. Many took to "social media" to try to bridge the gaps in the church's family life. While some stuck to simply broadcasting their services online, others have experimented with creative ways of expressing familiness - which in one case that I have enjoyed watching and listening – more familiness than it is normally possible to achieve by the ingredients of a Sunday service.

Livestreams and videos recordings have allowed us to personally experience a wider familiness with people known or unknown to us in other churches, by watching, listening and in some cases participating in church online get-togethers, and for me and my wife, Kate this has included Sutton Coldfield Baptist Church because her brother, Donald is there.

SUTTON COLDFIELD BAPTIST CHURCH

Along with online daily devotionals, weekly café church and "Questions of Life" discussions, their Sunday has had 3 livestreams at the times when their services would normally be held: 8.30am, 10.30am and 6.30pm

They did not try to replicate a church service. Instead they described their livestreams as "Call to Prayer" with prayers, testimonies, music and fun. It was hosted by Donald and another of the church team in what one might describe as a "chat-show" style, but that would not quite do it justice! While they included informal light-hearted conversation and some fun items, yet they covered serious issues, concerns and needs in prayer, always with a positive emphasis on relationship with Jesus and what he is able to do.

The online "congregation" was encouraged to take part in many ways such as:

- sending photos to serve as multi picture backdrop to the words of "How great Thou art".

- taking part in Paul's 60 second fun work-out – with his invitation for children to lead it on other occasions.

- videos of young and old taking part in a Family challenge.

- photos of people of the church community being prayed for – representing different services and professions.

- sharing family and personal testimonies – particularly in relation to the current situation.

- emailing while livestream is on – on anything , or in answer to a particular question "What do you always carry with you?" "What are you particularly thankful for this week?" "Do you have an encouraging scripture or prayer to share?"

- joining in prayers led by hosts with words on screen for participation by those watching, and also relevant Bible verses.

- much of the content was for all ages – with opportunities to draw a picture on the theme / or make something and take a photo – send it to be shown on the next livestream.

- songs were included – appropriate to whatever theme was being followed, with a wide mix of involvement of musicians and singers, joined together in the ways they can be using the internet technology.

One thing they use to very good effect is menti.com. The way it is used is that a number of questions can be listed which can be responded to by those watching the livestream. This can be by inserting an answer e.g. on Remembrance day – "who would you like to remember and thank God for today?" or by choosing an option e.g. "Today, for myself or someone else I am concerned about: finance / workload / mental health / health / relationships / isolation / tiredness, where the numbers choosing each one are shown in a bar graph. This means all can see the range of concerns that the church family has, individual participants can see that others share their concern and that they are being prayed for, the hosts can then lead a time for prayer for people in each category – and also see the extent that pastoral issues that are affecting their church family.

As you can see, the level of opportunity of active family participation in these livestreams is much greater than is experienced in "normal" church services.

You may have in your mind, "But where is the sermon? the preaching and teaching of God's Word?" Well, more detailed examples of that are done in separate online "broadcasts" – but for those who are able to see it, these "Call to Prayer livestreams" – with all their various linked items on a theme are actually a well thought out complete sermon in themselves – and to me more relevant and memorable than many sermons I have heard or I myself have preached!

It is strange that so much familiness can be experienced and appreciated when the church was not allowed to meet! And now that restrictions on meeting have been lifted, they are incorporating these different ways of family participation into their times together as a church family, while continuing their online connections.

THE LIVING ROOM

In conclusion, you may or may not remember that at the beginning of this book I posed the question, "Do people when they step in feel that they are coming into a meeting of brothers and sisters with their Father – into, as it were, the family's "living room"?

There is one place of church family which I am only able to visit once or twice a year, but where I am always remembered, recognised, accepted and treated as one of the family. Their care for me is seen in the regular messages I get from my daughter, Jane telling me of different ones asking how I am doing.

City Gates Church café in Soho, central London, "The Living Room" on Monday evenings is a home for the homeless with a free meal, friendship, refreshment, rest, Bible discussion, caring conversation and provision – in fact all the ingredients of familiness – not just <u>for</u> those who may lack a family of their own, but also wonderful expressions of familiness <u>by</u> them to one another, and to others, including me!

Simon gave his hand-written thoughts as follows:

I Like comming in The Living room café, city gates church because I Meet brothers + sisters in JESUS + allso Playing games. I allso like The food on a Monday night at 5pm. I allso like going to church on a Sunday at 10.30AM for praying before The service which is 11AM. and I like people to pray for me in the holey sprit and healing to.

Jane C.:

"I've been a coffee acquaintance in the Living Room café for years. It was a long journey for me. I gave up drugs – everything - ecstasy, magic mushrooms, opium - I used to use it and sell it. Not no more – I was a thief as well. Jesus has made me much better – made me come together as one... Jesus is helping me, and I won't give up like some people, but it's a long journey. The Bible classes are good and I have also felt welcome and safe."

Fernando:

"Some people don't have no family so it's like a family thing. It's a community. You can come if you want to. There's no restrictions. You can meet old and new friends. You feel free. Sometimes depression can be getting to you. Here we meet good people who volunteer to care for you. You can meet brothers and sisters from another parent. It's somewhere to go on Mondays from 5 to 9 and just be with yourself. You can play (board) games if you want to and feel free to talk to people if you have problems or issues. It feels like a loving community in a way. There's not a lot of places you can sit down and get tea or coffee and feel welcome always when you come through the door. I try to come every Monday whatever the situation is. It's been a long time on and off I've been coming to the Living Room. It's nice to sit down for a couple of hours."

Ernest (who rarely says anything more than a friendly greeting when he comes in): volunteered this observation: "Your daughter Jane is the mother of the family house – The Living Room. Christian fellowship is in the house."

SO WHAT'S NEXT?

We will each have a different personal answer to that question. Inspired by the words of Scripture, encouraged by examples of ways in which we could make a difference, perhaps like me, you are daunted by the challenge of seeing the necessary change which will remove the heavy religious overlay which so easily gets in the way of church family life.

I have been looking recently at the beginning of the book of Nehemiah. He was despondent about the situation of God's people at that time – and it showed on his face. The King he was serving noticed it, and asked him why he was so sad. Nehemiah told him, and then the King surprised him by asking, "So what is it that you want?"

Nehemiah said a quick prayer, and then told the King what he later described as "what my God had put in my heart to do…"

And he said, "because the gracious hand of my God was upon me…." he was given everything that he needed to fulfil much more than he could have ever hoped.

So while there are great challenges to face, as Father's children we can be assured that His gracious hand is upon us, and as we seek for "Church is Family" to become more of who we are, I want to leave you with that question, "What is it that you want?" with the expectation that there will be something that each one of us will be called to do, and for some, what Father puts in your heart will have a wide reaching influence beyond what you now think possible.

"Then I prayed to the God of heaven, and I answered…"

Graeme C. Young
graeme@youngresources.co.uk
www.youngresources.co.uk

Also by Graeme C. Young

Luke *into* Jesus is a practical commentary on Luke's Gospel, in a style designed to be particularly useful for followers of Jesus who are young in age or experience.

Luke *into* Jesus explores the book of Luke in 89 parts. Each part has notes about it in 4 sections:

- INFORMING:- explaining things that will help us in understanding the passage.

- INTRODUCING:- showing how the passage helps us to get to know Jesus better.

- INSPIRING:- seeing how the Holy Spirit is at work in the passage and in Jesus.

- INSTRUCTING:- discovering lessons we can put into practice in following Jesus.

Sunday school leader: We are using it with our primary school age children, focussing on one chapter as a topic guide each week. It has opened our eyes to the richness of Luke and is presented in short, easy to read chapters that are ideally pitched for this age group.

Young man: Very easy to read and comprehend. It is nice how various aspects of life at the time of Jesus are expounded on gradually as one reads through the book - really useful resource to introduce new Christians to.

Experienced Christian: A very readable book, such a lovely feel to it. I'm using it as a daily devotional. God has been showing me something new every day - what a blessing.

Cell Group Leader: I am using it with an adult cell group as it really engages people and is clear and direct.

Church elder: I've been using the book myself with a view to recommending it to the church to give to new communicants. I find it very user friendly and I like the layout. Having the historical background explained makes for easier understanding of the passage - simple explanations without being patronising to mature students.

Youth for Christ team member: I've got to say that it's got be one of the easiest books I have ever read. It is written in a way I really understand. I am really enjoying it, and once I have finished, I know a few people that would love to read it.

Church leader. I lent it to one of our church team to try out on a group of new believers, where we have been struggling to find something which is just right for them, and it is going down well with them.

83 year old: I am reading a section each morning and finding them very helpful and thought provoking.

Scripture Union camp leader: A unique book - in the format of a study guide or a commentary, but written in the style of an introductory book aimed at younger readers. Taking the time to work through Luke's Gospel guided by **Luke *into* Jesus** cannot fail to produce new insights into the Gospel, and most importantly deeper understanding of who Jesus is.

www.ingramcontent.com/pod-product-compliance
Lightning Source LLC
Chambersburg PA
CBHW032006040426
42448CB00006B/499